HINDU CHAPLAINCY

HINDU CHAPLAINCY

THE OXFORD CENTRE FOR HINDU STUDIES
&
VRIJE UNIVERSITEIT AMSTERDAM

Nicholas Sutton
Director of Continuing Education Department,
Oxford Centre for Hindu Studies

Vineet Chander
Coordinator for Hindu Life,
Hindu Chaplain to Princeton University

Shaunaka Rishi Das
Director, Oxford Centre for Hindu Studies,
Hindu Chaplain to Oxford University

A RECOGNISED INDEPENDENT CENTRE OF THE UNIVERSITY OF OXFORD

The Oxford Centre for Hindu Studies
Hindu Chaplaincy

Published by the Oxford Centre for Hindu Studies
13–15 Magdalen St, Oxford OX1 3AE, UK

www.ochsonline.org
Regd Charity No. 1074458

ISBN 978-1-9997644-0-1

CONTENTS

INTRODUCTION

Is there a need and place for Hindu chaplains today? If so, what challenges might they face? And what resources are available to them? This book addresses these questions and others by exploring Hindu chaplaincy in a modern, diaspora-conscious, western context.

Traditionally, a chaplain is a minister – or sometimes a lay representative of a religious tradition – who is attached to and serves a secular institution. Although chaplains play a number of roles, their primary function centres on the giving of pastoral care – offering faith-based emotional and spiritual support for people in their pain, loss, and anxiety, and sharing in their triumphs, joys, and victories.

The role of the religious chaplain is one that has emerged primarily from the Christian tradition, and specifically from Christianity's encounter with the modern world. This means that the role fits most easily with the vocation of the Christian clergy; it therefore may not appear to be immediately compatible with other religious traditions such as Hinduism. The main point to note here, however, is that Hindus in modernised societies have the same experience of life as everyone else and hence have similar psychological and spiritual needs. Thus all religious traditions would be well served to adopt the role of chaplain in a way that makes sense for them, and to draw upon the considerable resources each of them possesses in order to properly fulfil this vital role.

This does not mean, however, that we can simply ignore the significant differences that distinguish Hinduism from other religions. In the remainder of this brief introduction, we will highlight some of these differences, with a particular interest in examining how they provide unique challenges and opportunities to Hindu chaplains.

TRADITIONAL SOURCES OF PASTORAL AUTHORITY

A vital issue here is that of pastoral authority within the tradition – that is to say, those places in the faith that grant the chaplain his or her position for the practice of the vocation. For Christianity, the two main sources of such authority are the denominational or ecclesiastical hierarchies on the one hand, and sacred texts on the other. Most other major religions also locate pastoral authority in this way. Hinduism is different. Its lack of centralisation, institutional leadership, and tangible ecclesiastic structures has led many to question whether Hinduism ought to be considered a single faith at all – it might better be thought of, they would suggest, as a loosely bound 'family of faiths.'

Within what we conventionally refer to as Hinduism, there are groups or sects that have a clearly defined institutional hierarchy. The followers of the Swaminarayan faith are a good example of this; here the organisations have structures and hierarchies, institutional leaders have a clearly defined authoritative status, and a body of specific texts (perhaps even specific editions of those texts) are considered canonical. A Hindu chaplain who is a Swaminarayan religious leader and well-versed in their scriptures would certainly hold authority for those within that faith, but this would mean little to Hindus from a different tradition. Moreover, it is a relatively small percentage of Hindus who are adherents of any such sect, and hence for the majority of Hindus, institutional leaders do not have authority or indeed any guaranteed status as spiritual guides.

In Islam, Sikhism, and Christianity, we can recognise that the Qur'an, Granth Sahib, and Bible are recognised sources of authority; adherents will regard citations from these sacred texts as vital sources of instruction and are thus likely to accept chaplains who can demonstrate that they base their work on these texts. Is there a Hindu analogue? One might propose that, for Hindus, the Vedas hold a similar authoritative status, and to some extent this is accurate. However, the comparison does not seem to hold up when we move from the realm of theory to practice. The Vedas have been superseded and largely replaced by later texts, and thus play a relatively minor role in the beliefs and practices of most Hindus today. While most Hindus will acknowledge the authoritative status of the Vedas, very few are familiar with these texts and fewer still directly refer to them for guidance. Today the Vedas are used sparingly and largely for the performance of certain rituals; as we will discuss in later sessions, this ritual function will be of less significance for the chaplain.

We might then turn to other well-known scriptures as sources of authority, texts such as the Bhagavad-gita, Ramayana, or Mahabharata. Certainly, Hindus will look to such works for guidance, and these texts (the Gita in particular) have been increasingly viewed as having a 'pan-Hindu' significance. Still, a Hindu would likely engage with these texts in a different way than Christians look to the Bible, or Muslims turn to the Qur'an. Even while respecting and venerating a text, Hindus may not necessarily see it as holding absolute status. The Hindu canon is an open one, so that if a particular teacher attracts a following, his or her words and writings quickly come to hold the same elevated status as the ancient Sanskrit works. Even a text such as the Ramayana appears in several different versions, written and oral, and Hindus will frequently cite teachings or incidents from them that one will be unable to locate in the version attributed to Valmiki. All of this means that whilst sacred texts do hold a position of some authority, and can indeed be cited by Hindu chaplains for the purpose of offering guidance, they are not viewed as having the same absolute status and do not confer authority to a Hindu chaplain in the same way the Bible or Qur'an might for Christian or Muslim chaplains. The fact is that Hinduism has a vast array of texts that might be regarded as scripture, and the actual works that individuals or groups turn to depend, to a large extent, on the form of Hinduism they follow.

AN ALTERNATIVE MODEL OF PASTORAL AUTHORITY

Since articulating sources of scriptural and institutional authority is problematic in Hinduism, one might conclude that the religion is without any form of authority at all; that individuals are free to practise their religion in any way they see fit; and even that the faith is fundamentally incompatible with the concept of formal chaplaincy. This is not the case. Historically, Hindus have adhered to a highly regulated way of life and pattern of belief. They have created and maintained elaborate and complex systems of practice and ritual, preserved these systems through culture and language, and have passed these along to future generations through formal and informal education. Present day Hindus in parts of India have continued this in much the same way their forefathers did; outside of India, and in increasingly westernised spaces in India, Hindus uphold these traditions, beliefs, and practices in a remarkable way – even if the external appearances may have shifted dramatically.

Where then is the source of religious authority for contemporary Hinduism? We would suggest that the main location of pastoral authority within the Hindu tradition always seems to have been family and community, and that this remains the case today. Parents, elders, and other members of the extended family offered support and care to those who needed it; likewise, respected community leaders provided guidance and direction. On a local level, the community – and on an even more local level, the extended family – embodied the authority of the faith, scriptures, and teachings. This, then, becomes a model of pastoral authority that a Hindu chaplain might use to guide his or her own work. To the extent that a Hindu chaplain is playing the same role, he or she is able to serve as a surrogate 'family elder' or 'community leader' and embody (and draw from) the authority of the community and family.

Might such a model of chaplaincy overlap with some of the duties traditionally carried out by brahmins and temple priests? After all, brahmins and priests may once have fulfilled this role for local communities, as well. There is, of course, nothing that would preclude the possibility of a ritual priest also serving as a chaplain. Still, on a pragmatic level this seems unlikely. The priests' primary religious function seems always to have been as performers of ritual. In the Western world today this is even more the case, as the temple priests frequently have only a limited grasp of local languages and are unfamiliar with the challenges faced by most Hindus in these modernised societies. What about institutional religious leaders? Again, nothing would prevent such leaders from effectively serving as chaplains as well. In fact, many leaders – perhaps especially those who are younger and more conversant with the challenges faced by their members on the ground – will feel called to such work, and may make fine chaplains. Some leaders within particular Hindu sects will take up this role for fellow devotees, but as we have noted this will apply to only a relatively small minority of Hindus. Institutional leaders serving as chaplains for a broader, multi-denominational Hindu community on the other hand, will have to be especially careful to practise self-awareness as to which role they are playing at any given time, guard against their sectarian biases, and manage possible conflicts of interest. We will discuss this more explicitly later in the course.

At this point, let us note a possible objection: If we consider the chaplain to be no more than a stand-in for family elders and community leaders, then would this role not be redundant where the need is already fulfilled within families and communities? We might answer this in a few ways. First, we might concede that this may still be the case in tight-knit and traditional Hindu societies – villages in rural India, for instance – but that this is increasingly becoming the exception, rather than the rule. In the modern societies of the West, we can observe how traditional forms of family life are beginning to break down, and with them the traditional expressions of authority and guidance. The nuclear family is increasingly the norm, and families and communities are less close-knit. In such a milieu, a chaplain fulfils a role that is both necessary and lacking. Secondly, we might reflect on the fact that modern societies are also multi-faith societies, in which the adherents of other faith traditions engage with issues and approaches to their faith with the aid of chaplains. Hindus living alongside them will also seek to engage with these issues and explore the faith in ways that may never have been done within their own communities or families: a Hindu chaplain can help facilitate such exploration and engagement. Finally, we must acknowledge the reality that even within close-knit families and communities, there may be issues that arise which are so sensitive or particular that they require the intervention of a trusted advisor or caregiver outside of those structures. These might include, for instance, wrestling with gender and sexual identity, issues of abuse, anxiety around academic or vocational pressure, or crises of faith. In these instances, a Hindu chaplain would go beyond being a 'surrogate family elder' and play a uniquely important, and most likely, confidential role.

We explore the complexity involved in this Hindu model of chaplaincy later in the course. At this point, suffice it to say that for Hindus, the role of chaplain is primarily a modern one, but is nonetheless essential – especially for those who live in and have been acculturated by modern societies. The challenge is to work out how this new role is to be shaped, and how best to employ the resources Hinduism has to offer in fulfilling its main functions. The primary aim of this first section of the course will be to suggest how this can be done, and to provide guidance in seeking out the enormous range of resources that Hinduism makes available to a person who takes the time to study the tradition in greater detail.

To bring this introductory section to a close, let us now turn to two important ideas upon which we will build our exploration of Hindu chaplaincy: Hinduism's inherent diversity and pluralism on the one hand, and the overarching theme of dharma on the other.

DHARMA AMIDST DIVERSITY

As we have already noted, an important feature of Hinduism – and one that we must always be aware of – is the diversity of belief and practice that it embodies. Of course, all world religions manifest diversity to some extent, and we should be careful not to overemphasise the rigidity of the West or the multiplicity found in Hinduism. Still, it is undeniable that one encounters internal diversity within the Hindu traditions in a manner, and to an extent, that is unparalleled. A good example of this can be found in Hindu beliefs about the nature of God. For those who follow the Advaita philosophy of Shankaracharya, God is the totality of all existence, referred to as Brahman, and the path of religion is one based on the acquisition of knowledge or realisation of this fundamental truth. Other forms of Hinduism tend more towards devotion to a personal God, and place their emphasis on worship and divine love. Here the teaching focuses on surrender to that deity and the gift of grace, but there may be different views on whether that one supreme being is to be identified as Narayana, Shiva, Krishna, Rama, or Devi, the great goddess. Many Hindus believe that each of these forms of divinity is an aspect of the one God, but others hold to the view that the deity they worship stands as unique and above all others.

The implication of this diversity for the chaplain's work is fairly obvious. The Hindu chaplain tasked with caring for a broad Hindu community must be sensitive to the plurality of beliefs and practices he or she will encounter, and be keenly aware of the limits of his or her own expertise or authority – especially in encounters with Hindus whose beliefs or practices are different from, or even theologically at odds with, those of the chaplain's own. Moreover, a Hindu chaplain cannot make any presumptions regarding the particular beliefs an individual may hold, and must be prepared to listen carefully before attempting to give any form of spiritual or moral guidance. While this may be wise advice for any chaplain, it is especially important for Hindu chaplains to bear in mind.

Given this diversity, one might be tempted to conclude that – other than serving as a good listener or dispensing the most generic, vague advice – a Hindu chaplain would have little substance to offer. This is a mistaken point of view; as we explore the ways in which Hindu chaplains might draw on the tradition's resources, we also hope to demonstrate the continuing relevance of Hindu ideas. In many ways, Hinduism may model what many consider an ideal form of religion for the modern world, particularly as its internal diversity naturally gives rise to an inherent sense of tolerance and acceptance. This sense offers a robust challenge to bigotry and religious fundamentalism. Moreover, the major texts revered within the Hindu tradition, diverse as they may be, reflect upon the great issues of human existence in a manner that is both enlightening and profound. The task of the chaplain then, is to thoroughly understand these great works and to acquire the ability to apply their wisdom to the situations people face in the modern world.

A particularly important concept that, as we shall see, forms the foundation for the Hindu chaplain's work is the notion of dharma. Dharma seems to defy direct translation; in Indian religious literature, the word is used in a number of different senses. In philosophy it indicates the essential nature of any object, whilst for Buddhists and Hindus alike it can be taken as meaning the lifestyle and practices that lead to liberation from the world. The more usual sense of the term, however, is related to morality and living in a manner that is proper and righteous; we might best understand this as 'the proper way to live'. In previous ages this was often related to the duties specific to one's occupation, *varna* (caste), *ashram* (stage in life), or gender; today dharma is usually taken in the more general sense of living and acting in accordance with the moral order. The underlying belief is that by living in accordance with dharma an individual gains benefits either in this life or in the next birth, in accordance with the idea of karma.

In drawing from Hindu teachings about dharma, the chaplain will likely also engage with questions of soteriology – that is, with how the ultimate goal is perceived in Hinduism. The standard texts on Hinduism will uniformly proclaim that the goal of the religion is to achieve *moksha*, liberation from the cycle of rebirth, and will set forth varying teachings on how this is to be achieved, either through self-transformation via realised knowledge, or through the grace of a merciful and loving God. Nonetheless, the religious life of most Hindus is often focused primarily on existence in this world rather than escaping from its clutches. Even when the ending of rebirth is esteemed as a noble goal – especially as exemplified by a few exceptional saints among us – for most Hindus the honest (if unspoken) expectation is of continuing rebirth and gradually making spiritual advancement while acting righteously. Moreover, considerable attention is paid to what we might call 'pragmatic religion', which generally takes the form of rituals that will grant prosperity and well-being in this present lifetime. It is accepted that this form of religion is less exalted than the pure spirituality of *moksha-dharma*, but nonetheless much of the Hindu ritual is focused on these more mundane outcomes.

Dharma serves as a thread running across otherwise diverse Hindu traditions and teachings. But what does this dharma actually entail? There are ancient Sanskrit texts known as *dharma-shastras* that provide extensive lists of rules to be followed by the religious minded; someone unfamiliar with Hinduism might be tempted to identify these books as the definitive textbooks on dharma, and even read into them some idea of a 'Hindu Sharia'. Any such idea would, however, be wholly erroneous. Today these texts are virtually unknown within Hindu communities and have no practical authoritative status; a Hindu chaplain citing one of these texts would likely be met with blank stares or complete bewilderment. Moreover, some of the edicts contained within these works relate to caste and gender, and today most Hindus would find them unacceptable, and in direct conflict with their own understanding of dharma. Today the so-called *dharma-shastras* are little more than a historical footnote. That they have no real bearing on the modern Hindu's practice suggest the faith's tendency toward self-reform and evolution.

If these texts no longer have currency for Hindus, then where *do* adherents find guidance on living in accordance with dharma? Traditionally, the nature of dharma for an individual has been defined and enforced by family, caste, and community on the one hand, and by one's personal practice and experience, on the other. To some extent, this remains the case. In traditional contexts, the Hindu family is still a very tight unit and has a good degree of authority over individual lifestyles and morality. In modern societies, however, this authority is becoming increasingly eroded and challenged in a number of ways. Younger Hindus in particular tend to question what the basis of Hindu-specific ethical standards might be, or whether the religion imposes any such standards at all. This lack of clear rules and regulations poses obvious challenges to the Hindu chaplain tasked with providing guidance. At the same time, it also affords the chaplain with a great degree of flexibility and freedom as to how to engage with – and help others engage with – difficult questions or ethical dilemmas. For instance, a Hindu chaplain may exercise his or her judgement in determining how best to demonstrate 'ally-ship' to the LGBTQ community in general, and counsel LGBTQ Hindus specifically. By contrast, a Muslim chaplain – even one who privately holds progressive, egalitarian views – may be obliged to adopt a more conservative approach in order to remain in alignment with institutional and doctrinal restrictions imposed by the faith. Similarly, when questions relating to alcohol, diet, or sexual ethics arise, a Hindu chaplain enjoys wide latitude in determining and interpreting what the faith has to say in response, but also must grapple with the absence of clear-cut 'Hindu rules' governing the situation.

This reality is especially critical for Hindus in the modern era when the control of the family over younger generations is much less pronounced, and ethical standards need to be explained rather than merely asserted. What resources might the Hindu chaplain look for in determining, and articulating such standards? Although the regulations traditionally enforced by family and community have loosened, and the strictures of the ancient dharma texts have now been discarded (if indeed they were ever widely accepted), Hinduism retains a wealth of resources – teachings, key precepts, instructive narratives, allegories, and models – to be engaged with and implemented in one's life. In a critical passage of the Mahabharata, which we will look at in more detail later on, Krishna states overtly that dharma can never be reduced to a set of rules and regulations, as each situation in life is different. Dharma is whatever brings about the welfare of all beings, he says, and in each situation one must determine how this can best be achieved. What is the chaplain's place in such determination? Is the Hindu chaplain a sounding board, a dialogue partner, a voice of experience and wisdom, an advocate, a translator or interpreter of ancient texts? As our exploration of Hindu chaplaincy unfolds, it will be important to return to these questions.

Although Krishna offers the welfare of all beings as the singular standard by which dharma is assessed, Hindu teachings give us other suggestions that expand on, or add to, this idea – perhaps most notably the virtues of *ahimsa* (not harming), compassion for all, and honesty. These are not rules as such, but precepts and ideals to guide one toward the best course of action to be followed in any given situation. A key message of the Bhagavad-gita is the importance of one's motive for action; if our motivations are aligned with these precepts then it is almost certain that the action that follows will be in accordance with dharma, in spirit if not always in outcome. We will have more to say about dharma and Hindu ethics later.

To summarise, the role of Hindu chaplain is essentially a modern one, although it is by no means incompatible with tradition and is vitally important for Hindus living in the modern world. The world many Hindus live in today – especially in the west – is undeniably different from that of previous generations, and the religion has to adapt to meet the needs of modernity. One of these developments must be the establishing of the role of chaplains who are able to guide, help and advise, in a way that does justice to the integrity and diversity of Hindu beliefs and values, but at the same time is wholly relevant for people living in modern societies.

SHORT WRITTEN EXERCISES

1. What is dharma? How can Hindu chaplains best make use of ideas on dharma in their work?
2. How do Hindu ideas on religious authority differ from those of other major religions? What effect could this have on the work of the Hindu chaplain?

1. HINDU SPIRITUAL CARE

In the introductory session, we suggested that a chaplain could play a vital role in serving the needs of the Hindu community in contemporary, and especially global, settings. What would such a chaplain *do*? In this session, we begin to explore specific ways in which a chaplain might offer spiritual care to those he or she serves. After first offering a general examination of Hindu perspectives on care and compassion, we will highlight the role of the chaplain as a care-giver in a number of contexts: spiritual well-being, grief counselling, issues surrounding punishment and detention, and military defense.

To help us better understand the scope of chaplaincy needs in the Hindu community, and the diversity of approaches to spiritual care-giving, we might consider four examples that loosely correspond to the contexts we identify in this session: university chaplaincy, hospital chaplaincy, prison chaplaincy, and military chaplaincy. It should be noted, however, that spiritual care 'on the ground' is much more fluid and dynamic than these clear-cut categories might lead us to believe. In truth, a Hindu chaplain in one setting – and who might be accustomed to working in a particular context – is likely to come across situations that will require the offering of care in a different context as well. A Hindu chaplain serving in the military, for instance, might be called upon to help someone process the death of a loved one. A university chaplain may draw from Hindu wisdom on punishment and consequences in offering spiritual care to a student facing disciplinary charges or expulsion. Any number of combinations is possible, and we must thus remind ourselves to approach these contexts as helpful tools and not rigid formulae.

CARE AND COMPASSION

While the words 'care' and 'compassion' are clearly linked, if we consider them more carefully we might see that compassion is a state of consciousness whilst care is the natural result of that state of mind. In other words, one who has developed a compassionate outlook on the world will generally manifest that outlook as care. In considering the Hindu perspective, we must turn again to the concept of dharma; compassion for all beings is one of the fundamental precepts on which dharma is based. The Sanskrit word for compassion is *daya*, and this, along with *ahimsa* (not harming), is frequently cited as the essence of dharma.

Hence at this point we need to return to our previous discussion of dharma and go a little further in determining the ethical basis of Hindu teachings. Hindus often prefer to refer to their religion as Sanatana Dharma, a term that we also find used in some of the ancient Sanskrit texts, most notably in the Mahabharata. So let us start by looking at some extracts from the Mahabharata, which explain the centrality of *daya* and *ahimsa* to Sanatana Dharma. Before turning to the text, however, it may be helpful to clarify what Hindus mean by 'non-harming' when they evoke the concept of *ahimsa.* At first glance, it might be tempting to see *ahimsa* merely as a negative injunction to avoid speech or action that explicitly causes pain to others. It is, however, much more than this. A simple example will suffice to make the point. If I walk past a lake and see a child in difficulty, I might decide that I will not take any action because I am wearing a new pair of trousers that would be ruined in any rescue attempt. One might assume that I have not infringed on the principle of *ahimsa* because I have not directly harmed anyone. This of course would be an erroneous and dangerous misunderstanding of *ahimsa.* For Hindus, *ahimsa* relates both to positive and negative actions, and must involve direct action to alleviate suffering as well as avoiding action that causes harm. In this way we can observe the close relationship that exists between *ahimsa* and compassion.

Here are a few quotations from the Mahabharata that reveal the close connection between compassion and dharma.

adrohah sarva-bhuteshu
karmana manasa gira
anugrahas cha danam cha
satam dharmah sanatanah

> Never displaying malice towards any living being through actions, thoughts, or words; acts of kindness, and giving in charity; this is the Sanatana Dharma adhered to by righteous persons (Mahabharata, 3.281.34).

This is a verse spoken by Savitri to Yama, the god of death, in a story told in the Mahabharata. Her whole discourse on dharma is worthy of fuller consideration, and, according to the story, it was so wonderful to listen to that it persuaded Yama to restore Savitri's dying husband to life. Here Savitri offers a threefold definition of dharma based on the principles of not harming, kindness, and charity. This provides us with a workable definition of Sanatana Dharma, and one can clearly perceive how care and compassion are central to that understanding.

sarvam priyabhyupagatam
dharmam ahur manishinah
pasyaitam lakshanad desam
dharmadharme yudhisthira

> The wise say that dharma is whatever is based on love for all beings. This is the characteristic mark that distinguishes dharma from *adharma* [its opposite], Yudhishthira. (Mahabharata, 12.251.24)

'Love for all beings' is a very high ideal to aspire toward, but the point here is clearly made. From the Hindu perspective, compassion cannot be separated from dharma, and dharma is an intrinsic part of spiritual consciousness. In other words, compassion is not a quality one simply adopts but is a mark of one's spiritual development. We will say a little more on this important point later on.

anukrosho hi sadhunam
su-mahad-dharma-lakshanam
anukroshas cha sadhunam
sada pritim prayacchati

> Amongst righteous persons, compassion is seen as the great characteristic mark of dharma; and compassion is always a source of delight for the righteous. (Mahabharata, 13.5.23)

This verse states directly that compassion is the key criterion that helps us to understand the true nature of dharma. On the basis of this statement, one might even assert that dharma, and hence Hindu spirituality, is focused on the ideal of universal compassion, which will be reflected in the care and concern one shows for others. Hence one who feels compassion and one who provides care for others is, on one level at least, the ideal Hindu – the perfect follower of Sanatana Dharma. An important word here is *lakshana*, which means the distinguishing characteristic. In this case it indicates that compassion is what marks a mood or action out as being in accordance with dharma.

ata urdhvam pravakshyami
niyatam dharma-lakshanam
ahimsa lakshano dharmo
himsa chadharma-lakshana

> Now then I will speak of what has been established as the characteristic mark of dharma. Ahimsa is the characteristic mark of dharma, whilst *himsa* is the characteristic mark of *adharma*. (Mahabharata, 14.43.19)

Here the same word, *lakshana*, is used again in relation to dharma, but in this verse it is ahimsa that is designated as the *dharma-lakshana*, the characteristic mark showing that thoughts, words, or deeds are in accordance with Hindu dharma. There is no real contradiction, however, for as we have already seen, ahimsa and compassion represent virtually the same idea of relieving the suffering of others, and are therefore intimately related to caring actions.

These quotations are just a small selection taken from many that could be used, but what they do show is that care and compassion are fundamental to the Hindu understanding of Sanatana Dharma. In fact, one might even conclude that without compassion, dharma cannot truly be present. This then can be taken as the Hindu ethical perspective, but it is also closely related to Hindu ideas of spirituality. The medieval saint Sanatana asserts that one who dedicates himself to worshipping God is referred to as *para-duhkha-duhkhi*, suffering at the suffering of others – a remarkable parallel to the literal definition of the English word compassion ('to suffer with'). At the same time, the Mahabharata and other texts are unequivocal in insisting that the mood of compassion is an essential part of spiritual realisation. Here is another quotation from the Mahabharata that makes that point abundantly clear.

grihastho brahmachari cha
vanaprastho 'tha va punah
ya icchen moksham asthatum
uttamam vrittim ashrayet

abhayam sarva-bhutebhyo
dattva naishkarmyam acharet
sarva-bhuta-hito maitrah
sarvendriya-yato munih

> Whether he be a householder, unmarried student, or a hermit living in the forest, anyone who wishes to achieve liberation from rebirth must adhere to the most perfect way of life.
>
> Only when he bestows the gift of fearlessness on all living beings can the sage achieve freedom from karma. He should act for the welfare of all beings, show kindness to all, and bring his senses under control. (Mahabharata, 14.46.17–18)

The significance of these verses is that they show that compassion is not merely related to dharma or ethics in this world, but is also an integral part of the Hindu path to liberation from rebirth – the way to *moksha*. This carries the discussion to a different level, revealing that ideas of care and compassion permeate all areas of Hindu thought, be they related to life in this world or to gaining release from it.

Up to this point, it has been suggested that the duty of care arises naturally alongside the quality of compassion. But what about when one simply does not feel that compassion? We are, after all, not perfect saints such as those referred to in the Mahabharata. So if we do not feel that instinctive mood described there, how should we broach the question of care provision? Here we must introduce the notion of a *karma-yoga*, which is central to contemporary Hinduism and elaborately described in the Bhagavad-gita. In the opening chapters of that work, Krishna explains to Arjuna that the actions we perform should be strictly in accordance with the precepts of dharma, and should be undertaken without selfish desire. This desireless action in pursuit of dharma is what is referred to by the Gita as *karma-yoga*. Extending this idea, we can see that even if compassion is limited or absent, the duty of care to others persists as the ideal mode of action, in line with Hindu teachings on duty. We will revisit this idea of *karma-yoga* a number of times, as it is of great significance in the fulfilment of the chaplain's role.

In more recent years, a number of teachers, perhaps most notably Swami Vivekananda and Mahatma Gandhi, have taken up this idea of expressing dharma through selfless acts of care. Vivekananda was an ardent proponent of the Hindu doctrine of Advaita, as originally set forth in the Upanishads and then more systematically by Shankaracharya (788–820AD). The Advaita school of thought teaches the unity of all existence and most especially the oneness of all beings. Citing Upanishadic aphorisms such as *sarvam khalv idam brahma*, 'all this is Brahman alone', and *tat tvam asi*, 'this (Brahman) is what you are', Shankara argued that the distinctions between one person and another are unreal. We are all Brahman; we are all one existence. Swami Vivekananda took this teaching a stage further by arguing that if one accepted the idea of absolute unity, then it should be expressed by actions performed on behalf of others. In other words, if you truly adhere to the ideas of Advaita Vedanta, then this will be apparent in the instinctive sense of compassion you feel, and through acts of care you perform. Here are some quotations from Swami Vivekananda that serve to illustrate his ideas of constructive Vedanta.

> A hundred thousand men and women, fired with the zeal of holiness, fortified with eternal faith in the Lord, and nerved to a lion's courage by their sympathy for the poor and the fallen and the

> downtrodden, will go the length and breadth of the land, preaching the gospel of salvation, the gospel of help, the gospel of social raising up – the gospel of equality.
>
> ***
>
> First bread and then religion. We stuff them too much with religion, when the poor fellows have been starving. No dogmas will satisfy the cravings of hunger. There are two curses here, first our weakness, secondly our hatred, our dried up hearts. You may talk doctrines by the millions, you may have sects by the hundreds of millions; aye, but it is nothing until you have the heart to feel; feel for them as your Veda teaches you, till you find they are parts of your bodies, till you realise that you and they, the poor and the rich, the saint and the sinner, are all parts of the One Infinite Whole, which we call Brahman.
>
> ***
>
> No man, no nation, can hate others and live.... Take care how you foster that idea. It is good to talk glibly about Vedanta, but how hard to carry out its least precepts!

These quotations represent just a small sample of Swami Vivekananda's ideas, but we can see clearly from them how he translates the ancient doctrine of Advaita Vedanta, the unity of all existence, into an assertion of the need for universal compassion and universal care for others. This is a vitally important addition to the Hindu understanding of life in this world, and especially relevant to those – like chaplains – charged with the role of care-giver.

Traditionally, the duty of care in Hindu society would have been carried out within the extended family and the wider community, particularly with regard to those especially vulnerable or in need of help such as the sick, the elderly, widows and orphans. Today, however, the rigidity of family structures is relaxing and it is within this context of change that the need for formal Hindu chaplaincy arises. This is a new role for Hindus, shaped by the exigencies of modern living, but in many ways it is not wholly innovative. As we have discussed, the Hindu tradition provides the essential values to be honoured and implemented in a changing social environment. This though has always been the situation; throughout history, Hindu society has been subjected to major changes and has had to adapt to new situations whilst preserving and enshrining ancient values. Today our task is to do the same, by determining how best to implement those great precepts and values that have been handed down to us over the generations.

Read through the following extract from the Mahabharata, which we have selected because it reveals the centrality of compassion to the concept of dharma. At times religion insists on the primacy of the other world over concern for people's welfare in the here and now. This has certainly been the case in India where the priestly class has often appeared to be committed only to ritual, and thereby uninterested in the welfare of the poor and oppressed. This story from the Mahabharata reflects on this precise issue and emerges with a response; it is hence one that the chaplain may find useful for guidance on the importance of care and compassion.

The setting is the aftermath of a great battle, and we find Yudhishthira filled with regret over the tragic loss of life, seeing himself as sinful because of the violence he has taken part in. The sage Vyasa comforts him by insisting that everything that occurred was due to destiny alone, and then instructing that he should perform an elaborate Vedic ritual, which will serve as atonement for any sinful act he may have performed.

Yudhishthira accepts this advice and arranges for the performance of an *asvamedha-yajna*, one of the most complex ritual ceremonies prescribed in the Vedic texts. This ritual requires the participation of innumerable priests and is very costly to perform because of the golden implements used by the priests to make their offerings.

We join the narrative at the conclusion of the ceremony when Yudhishthira has just received the great blessing he has been seeking to eradicate any trace of sin. The passage presented here is a summary of the content of Chapter 92 of Book 14 of the Mahabharata.

The golden mongoose

> Now hear about a most wonderful incident that occurred when the ritual was complete. After the priests had been rewarded and the poor and destitute all fed, a blue-eyed mongoose with a golden side suddenly appeared there and began to speak to Yudhishthira and his brothers. 'O you kings,' the mongoose said, 'this great ritual cannot equal a small quantity of flour given away by a brahmin who was about to break his fast.'
>
> When they heard these words the priests came forward and began to question the extraordinary creature, 'Who are you? Where have you come from? How can you criticise the wonderful ceremony we have just completed? Every aspect of this ritual performance was perfectly enacted exactly as directed by the Vedas, the priests have been fully rewarded and generous gifts of charity given away. And yet you appear very wise and you have a form like one of the gods so please explain these words you have spoken.'
>
> When questioned in this way, the mongoose replied as follows, 'In the sacred land of Kurukshetra there lived a pious brahmin who fasted every

day until the evening when he would take just a small quantity of simple food. There was then a famine in the land and the brahmin and his family could never get enough to feed themselves. On some days they had nothing at all to eat. One day during this time of hardship, the brahmin managed to obtain a quantity of flour barely sufficient to provide a meal for himself and his family.

The meal was prepared but just as the family were about to eat a hungry guest arrived at their home begging for a morsel to eat. All the family stood to welcome this stranger and respectfully requested him to come in and sit down. As the man was starving and on the verge of death, each of them, beginning with the father, gave up his or her portion of the food and gave it to this man in order to ease his suffering. When the guest had eaten all the food available and the family was left with nothing, a light appeared in the sky, flowers rained down and Dharma, the god of virtue, descended to earth to bestow his blessings upon them.

Dharma then spoke the following words, 'My blessings upon you, for your acts of kindness have made you glorious in this world and amongst the gods as well. As long as one retains one's dedication to giving in charity, one's dharma will never fade away. Through your virtue and your adherence to the principles of dharma you have conquered the world and your fame will last forever.'

The brahmin and his family then entered a celestial chariot and ascended to the realm of the gods. At that time I emerged from the hole in the ground where I lived and ran across the ground outside the brahmin's house so that a few particles of the flour given in charity touched one side of my body. It is as a result of my contact with the food given

> in charity to a needy person that you see me now possessing this form with one side that is golden.
>
> Now whenever I hear that religious acts are being undertaken, I go to that place immediately in the hope that the whole of my body may become golden, and it is for this reason that I have come here today. I remain, however, unchanged, and it was for this reason that I stated earlier that the ceremony you have enacted here could not equal the simple act of charity performed by a man of kindness. It was by the grains of flour that I became golden and clearly this great ritual, wonderful as it was, could not match the piety of those grains.' Having spoken these words, the mongoose became silent and disappeared from that place.

Throughout the religions of the world, we often encounter this tension between ritual and pure virtue; it becomes particularly acute when we encounter a person who has no interest in formal religion and yet is consistently charitable and benevolent towards others. In terms of the definition of dharma we have encountered here, such a person meets the criteria more fully than another who might speak constantly of religion but whose compassion towards others is less evident.

This story makes a profound point, placing virtue and compassion above even the most elaborate of ritual acts. This is, the story suggests, what dharma really means. The passage does not entirely dismiss the value of ritual acts but it is unequivocal in its assertion that compassion is the true heart of dharma. We would be remiss not to take note, however, that at some later date an interpolation was added to the text of the Mahabharata, attempting to show that the mongoose was in fact an evil being that entered the sacrificial arena to spread doubt and confusion and thereby discredit the pristine, ritualistic Vedic religion. There can be little doubt that this addition to the text was made by some member of the priestly order unable to accept the precedence given to virtue over ritual, which the narrative so clearly espouses. The mere fact that these priests would see the need to rehabilitate the story speaks volumes to just how contentious the tension can be.

The Hindu chaplain must especially negotiate this tension between ritual and virtue, as experienced by one chaplain:

> I served as a chaplain working in a hospital attempting to administer care to Hindu patients and their families. While many appreciated my offering of spiritual care, others seemed more focused on their ritual needs. In one instance, the family of the patient became visibly upset by my presence, considering the arrival of a 'Hindu priest' at the bed-side of their ailing (but still very much alive) relative a suggestion that last rites were in order! In another case, the wife of a patient in his final hours requested the chaplain's assistance in gathering together the items typically used in Hindu dying rituals, such as holy water from the Ganges and *tulsi* leaves, but spoke about her feelings of grief and loss hesitatingly and only as an afterthought.
>
> In another encounter, the family of a terminally ill patient asked me to help find a local ritual priest to carry out the rituals for the dying. As orthodox brahmins, originally hailing from Tamil Nadu, it was critical to the family members that the ritual was conducted only by a South Indian priest from a priestly hereditary background – even if such a priest did not share their theological orientation. They respectfully (but firmly) declined any engagement with me (despite my sharing their theological outlook) beyond asking me to connect them with the ritual priest.

We will return to the chaplain's engagement with ritual later in the course; at this point we can simply note that the relationship between ritual and virtue must be carefully and thoughtfully navigated.

THE CONTEXT OF SPIRITUAL WELL-BEING

An obvious context within which the Hindu chaplain serves as a care-giver is in his or her capacity to guide others to lead spiritually healthy, fulfilling lives. The chaplain can play an invaluable role in helping Hindus to reflect upon – and actively work on improving – the quality of their lives and relationships, the development of self-awareness, their capacity for empathy, and their sense of contentment.

When we turn to the subject of spiritual well-being, we are inevitably drawn back to the consideration of the enormous diversity that exists within Hindu religious teachings. As we have hinted at in the introduction, while this diversity offers the chaplain a wealth of resources and interpretations to draw from, it can also be problematic. A Hindu chaplain cannot always know what those in his or her care actually believe, or which form of Hinduism they follow. Hence the first priority is to listen and to reflect. While this is true of chaplains generally, the necessity becomes even more acute for the Hindu chaplain in light of the diversity of Hindu teachings.

From the standpoint of chaplaincy, spiritual well-being is ultimately rooted in one's sense of self, one's engagement with others, and one's feelings of connectedness to (or alienation from) divinity. At this point of our discussion, it therefore becomes essential to say a few words about Hindu metaphysics and theology – that is, ideas about the nature of God and the nature of the self – for without some knowledge of this subject we cannot meaningfully explore how a chaplain might give effective guidance. There can be no doubt that the greater the knowledge the chaplain possesses, the more effective any such counselling will be.

So let us start with a brief summary of Hindu theology, and a consideration of how this is reflected in the more popular forms of the religion.

Within mainstream Hindu thought, one can observe a range of theological perspectives, and some of these are not directly compatible. The system known as Advaita Vedanta is widely admired by Hindu intellectuals and many Hindus will say that this is the way of thinking they follow. Advaita literally means 'non-dual' and we can find evidence of this perspective in the Upanishads and perhaps in the Bhagavad-gita as well. It was, however, Shankaracharya who systematised the Advaita system and provided in his writings a clear appraisal of what it is asserting. Essential for Shankara's system is the idea of levels or degrees of 'realness'. The world we see and experience, and our sense of being an individual, represents one level of reality: but not the absolute reality. The world is not unreal, but neither is it real in an absolute sense. The absolute reality is Brahman alone, the one supreme truth that exists without change or division. Our sense of self is a form of illusion for we are Brahman (*aham brahmasmi*, in the Brihad Aranyaka Upanishad) and the goal of our spiritual quest is to fully realise that truth, thereby transcending individual existence and the suffering that goes with it. This can be achieved either by immersing one's mind in the teachings of the Upanishads and other sacred texts or by the practice of meditational yoga, seeking thereby to explore the innermost reality of one's existence.

This is just a brief summary of some of the principal elements of Shankara's teachings, and the chaplain would be well advised to explore the subject in greater detail. The points made here do, however, serve to give some insight into one of the ways in which spiritual well-being can be promoted. When reflecting on the Advaita Vedanta, the question naturally arises as to the existence or otherwise of a personal God who is active in the world. Buddhists and Jains argue against the notion of any such supreme deity, but Shankara does not go quite that far. Rather he affirms the concept of a personal God who controls this world and responds to prayer and other devotional acts, and the efficacy of such worship by the devotee – but only to an extent. A God distinct from the worshiper and possessing attributes (*saguna brahman*) is real only inasmuch as he or she is a part of this world and this contingent reality. At the point of ultimate realisation, all such concepts are transcended, for there can be no distinction between the self and the deity worshipped. All is one, all is Brahman.

Other branches of the Hindu tradition do, however, take a rather different point of view, and there are a number of great teachers of Hinduism who are at complete loggerheads with Shankaracharya, seeing him as a philosophical opponent of the pure theism they advocate. Here we might notice individuals such as Ramanujacharya (1018?-1138), Madhvacharya (1238–1307), Vallabhacharya (1479–1531), Chaitanya Mahaprabhu (1486–1534) and Swaminarayan (1781–1830). These teachers, and many others, emphasised the distinction between the personal God and the individual self, and taught that the deity they revered was ultimate and absolute, not merely a part of contingent reality. They proclaimed that Vishnu, or Narayana, was the one supreme God, and taught that worship of God (*bhakti*) is the highest form of religion. Moreover, Vishnu is a merciful, loving deity who blesses his worshippers, protects them from evil, and showers them with gifts of divine grace. Vishnu also appears as avatars such as Krishna and Rama and many Vaishnavas tend to focus more on these manifestations of the divine than on the original deity himself.

In some Hindu traditions, particularly those with roots in the South of India, devotees direct worship and devotion towards Shiva. These can be designated as Shaivites. In Bengal and in other parts of India there are some for whom the primary object of devotion is Devi, the supreme goddess, generally named as Parvati, Durga, or Kali.

This brief summary of the many and varied expressions of devotional Hinduism again serves to demonstrate the diversity that chaplains will have to come to terms with in their work; again, we must emphasise the importance of listening to individuals before guidance and help can be effectively offered. The chaplain might have occasion to offer guidance, but he or she serves his or her people rather than being their guru or leader – a critical but subtle distinction that we will explore in more detail later in the course.

In terms of spiritual well-being, the various forms of Hindu religious thought offer various avenues of approach; a common factor is that they aim to help the person being counselled to become aware of that which is greater than this world. This may be the significance, spiritual or ethical, of living a life in accordance with dharma; it may be the understanding of one's own identity as eternal and absolute rather than limited and temporary; or it may be an acceptance of the love, mercy, and grace, of a personal God. More likely, it will be a combination of these that together offer a means to reduce stress, provide comfort in times of adversity, and enable a degree of transcendence that can take any person some way beyond 'the slings and arrows of outrageous fortune.'

Whatever the particular theological beliefs an individual may hold, by taking up the path of dharma with enthusiasm and making the duty to help others an integral part of a person's life, he or she is very likely to experience a feeling of well-being and personal value. This will be the case both for those who are intensely devoted to God, or for those who have little faith of that kind. Dharma itself, Hindu teachings suggest, is a positive force both for the giver and the recipient of kindness and acts based on compassion.

Living an ethical life and cultivating an awareness of something greater than oneself is a part of the approach to spiritual well-being in Hinduism, but it is not the final word. In fact, the 'this-worldly' approach to the faith is balanced by the more metaphysical approach taken by teachers of

Vedanta, particularly in the Advaita Vedanta tradition. Here the revelation is that we are not limited individuals, confined within a body and mind which must undergo suffering, but rather we are a part of something greater, the supreme reality that is Brahman. Hence our time in this world may be troubled, and we will certainly encounter a degree of misery and hardship, but this is not the full picture. If we try to realise our higher identity, then the stress and suffering of this world become less overwhelming. An often quoted mantra of the Upanishads states, *aham brahmasmi*, I am Brahman. This sense of higher identity, along with an understanding of the soul's eternal nature, can help Hindus maintain perspective and non-attachment, and can thus be effective in alleviating our troubles and in promoting a sense of spiritual well-being.

This approach is certainly not the final word on Hindu approaches to well-being. Whilst many Hindus may hold to the Vedantic ideals and metaphysical understanding at a theoretical level, the reality of the lived religion is almost universally devotional. Even Shankara, the greatest exponent of Advaita Vedanta, concedes that on the level of conventional reality, devotion is the most effective route to spiritual connection. And, as we have discussed, other schools hold that devotion is not merely a means on the conventional plane, but is the nature of our eternal relationship with the Divine.

Thus devotion is an integral part of addressing well-being from a Hindu perspective. The particular expressions of devotion and chosen deities will vary based on regional, linguistic, and sectarian differences. For instance, amongst the diaspora communities living in the Western world, those of Gujarati or Punjabi background are likely to hold Krishna, Rama, or Durga as their main objects of devotion. South Indians, on the other hand, may be more likely to give particular attention to the forms of Vishnu or Shiva. Nonetheless, most Hindus hold to the view that these different deities are all manifestations of the one supreme truth, and hence there should be no sectarian divisions between the worshippers of different manifestations of God. In many cases, individuals will worship all forms of the deity and observe their festivals in turn, such as Sri Krishna Janmashthami, Maha Shiva Ratri, or Nava Ratri in celebration of the Goddess.

With this context as a backdrop, we can better appreciate the role of devotional practice in spiritual well-being. Hindus tend to express faith in God through personal and communal acts of devotion, and the chaplain can draw from this tendency as a resource. Hindu traditions carry a strong and widespread belief that the merciful God will watch over those who are devoted to Him, and will act as their saviour and protector. This sense of not having to face the world alone is a source of immense comfort, particularly in times of stress, grief, or anxiety. The constant presence and support of God is, in fact, one of the primary themes that emerge from the Bhagavad-gita. Krishna takes the role of the chariot driver of his friend, Arjuna and guides him through his darkest hour, which seems to suggest that God similarly makes himself available to guide and direct *us* in *our* darkest hour. Throughout the text, Krishna emphasises his unwavering support and assistance; he even exhorts Arjuna (and the reader) to 'be free of worry or fear' (*ma suchah*) and depend on him. In a particularly moving passage, he identifies himself as the indwelling Lord who frees his devotee from darkness and ignorance and offers enlightenment:

tesham evanukampartham
aham ajñana-jam tamah
nashayamy atma-bhava-stho
jñana-dipena bhasvata

> I am situated within their existence, and due to my compassion for them (devotees), I destroy the darkness that arises from ignorance, using the effulgent lamp of knowledge. (Bhagavad-gita, 10.11)

Here the word *anukampa*, part of the compound phrase in line one, is especially significant in that it suggests that God is compassionate toward the living beings of this world, and acts on their behalf from his position within the hearts of all.

Likewise, at the very conclusion of that scripture we find these words spoken by Krishna to the devoted Arjuna:

sarva-dharman parityajya
mam ekam sharanam vraja
aham tvam sarva-papebhyo
mokshayishyami ma suchah

> Setting aside all other forms of dharma, you can seek shelter with me alone. I will deliver you from all the evils of the world. Do not fear. (Bhagavad-gita, 18.66)

Here, Krishna not only offers re-assurance and comfort – promising that he will protect us from evils and again allaying our fear – but he also explicitly offers himself as the exclusive shelter and refuge for his devotees in the phrase *mam ekam sharanam vraja*. This idea is echoed in the main prayer of the followers of Vallabhacharya: *shri krishna sharanam mama* ('Sri Krishna is my shelter'). Many adherents of this tradition repetitively chant this prayer (often on wooden prayer beads, or *jap-mala*) as a meditation practice.

These words and others like them can bring great comfort to those who suffer, and the idea of the overarching mercy and kindness of God is a vitally important source of spiritual well-being that the chaplain can draw upon in virtually any situation.

A second resource available to Hindu chaplains under the heading of spiritual well-being is mindfulness practice drawn from Hinduism's yoga teachings.

Mindfulness is becoming increasingly valued in the secular arena. For instance, academic studies have demonstrated that those who practise mindfulness are likely to relieve stress and to combat depression and anxiety without absolute dependence on medication.

The Hindu tradition and its texts offer the chaplain a wealth of resources. Patañjali's Yoga Sutras and the sixth chapter of the Bhagavad-gita, for instance, share techniques of meditation that emphasise mental equilibrium and spiritual well-being. Here we should take note that although many yoga courses today mainly consist of physical exercises and postures, the older traditional texts assert that yoga is primarily a practice of the mind and the spirit, rather than the body, though of course the three are never entirely distinct from one another.

The techniques referred to in these ancient texts are primarily related to bringing the wandering mind under direct control, so that it can be fixed on a single point. According to the Yoga Sutras, the practice of yoga is essentially *chitta-vritti-nirodha*, stilling the movements of the mind, and the Bhagavad-gita describes a very similar process. For both these texts, the ultimate goal is the direct realisation of the soul, the *atman*, within the body. Needless to say, this is by no means an easy goal to achieve, but, for our purposes, the attempt on its own can be highly therapeutic and effective in promoting spiritual well-being. Again, contemporary scientific research seems to verify this.

Hindu chaplains can help those they are counselling to find a practice that honours the tradition but is also easy to implement and sustain. For instance, one might adopt a relatively simple technique in which the practitioner adopts a sitting posture that is steady and comfortable; this can either be on a mat or on a chair if that seems more suitable. Then one begins by breathing in and out in a steady, regulated manner, and if possible concentrating on the movement of the breath inwards and outwards. Then the process of controlling the mind begins. The chaplain might recommend that the practitioner use a word or mantra. These can be the tantric mantras such *klim, aim, srim,* or *hrim,* or else those used in devotional Hinduism such as *om namo narayanaya, om namo bhagavate vasudevaya,* or *om namah shivaya.* The practice then consists of attempting to keep the mind fixed on the words of the mantra and overcoming the innate tendency of the mind to drift into various patterns of thought. As mentioned before, the original aim of this technique was to grant the adept direct perception of the true self, but it is well attested that even a limited amount of practice can bring immense (and often immediate) benefit in terms of spiritual and mental well-being. The chaplain can play an invaluable role in helping Hindus to identify meaningful practices from within their own traditions and then delicately adapt those practices from their original aims to address the issues facing Hindus today.

Much more can be said of Hindu approaches to caring for one's spiritual well-being. What we can observe from this brief discussion is that the Hindu tradition has an enormous range of resources available that can contribute towards the spiritual well-being of each individual who seeks contact with the chaplain. As we have seen, Hinduism's approach to spiritual well-being largely rests on seeing something in the world beyond the here and now, beyond the immediate experiences of life. This may be through dedication to the concept of dharma, ensuring that one's thoughts, words, and deeds are beneficial to others, and bring no harm to the world around us. It may be through an understanding of Advaita Vedanta, gaining awareness of the idea that this existence is only limited and temporary, whilst our true identity is eternal and divine. Or it may be through intense devotion to God in the form of Rama, Krishna, Shiva, or Parvati, believing intensely in the love and shelter given by the deity, and the ability of the worshipper to reciprocate that love. The Hindu tradition has innumerable resources to help one gain the sense of transcendence that is the key to spiritual well-being, and the chaplain can play a uniquely important role in helping Hindus to seek out, adopt, and make use of those resources.

At this point, it may be necessary to clarify a misunderstanding that often arises when discussing Hinduism's emphasis on transcendence. That Hindus link spiritual well-being with transcendence of this world does not mean to suggest that every person has to become a sadhu, saint, or mendicant – renouncing the world for the religious life. On the contrary, Hindu teachers consistently stress that there should be some degree of balance between the world we must live and work in, and the higher matters revealed by Hindu teachings. The Hindu tradition asserts that there are four main goals of life to be pursued: designated *kama*, fulfilling material desires; *artha*, acquiring wealth or prosperity; *dharma*, living in a way that is righteous; and *moksha*, the spiritual path that leads eventually to liberation from rebirth. The key point is that there should be balance in life as one engages with and pursues each of these goals. There is nothing wrong with fulfilling one's desires, or seeking prosperity, but these aspirations should be balanced against righteous and compassionate living, and an awareness of the higher spiritual existence. Above all else, it is this balance of goals that brings one a sense of spiritual well-being, and a Hindu chaplain must be careful to convey this. Of course, in offering care to the precious few who are genuinely called to pursue the monastic life, the chaplain may need to draw on additional resources from Hinduism's renunciate traditions; these cases will almost certainly be the exception, however, and not the rule.

Here are two short episodes from the Bhagavata Purana that illustrate the importance of spiritual well-being in dealing with life's tribulations. The first is from Book 3, Chapter 1, verses 6–16.

> Shuka said: 'Because of his desire to support his wicked sons, King Dhritarashtra allowed the house of shellac to be set on fire so that the Pandava brothers would be killed. Similarly he did not prevent

Duhshasana from dragging the weeping Draupadi into the assembly, pulling her by the hair. Yudhishthira was cheated in the gambling match but because he was always truthful, he went to live in the forest. When he returned, Dhritarashtra refused to allow him to rule over the kingdom that was his by right. Sri Krishna was sent to the Kaurava assembly by Yudhishthira in order to negotiate a peace agreement, but the king would not listen to his righteous words. When Dhritarashtra invited his brother Vidura to give him advice on matters, the latter gave Dhritarashtra wise advice that was in accordance with dharma.'

Vidura said:'You must restore the proper share of the kingdom to Yudhishthira now that he has suffered so much being exiled to the forest. You must fear Yudhishthira and his warlike brothers, the mighty Bhima in particular. Krishna, who is the blessed Lord, has accepted the Pandava brothers as his relatives and allies. He is now with the Pandavas along with all the Yadus and his powerful friends. You give support to your wicked son, Duryodhana, who despises Sri Krishna, and this policy will strip you of your opulence. You should immediately give up this foolish policy, which will bring misfortune to all your family.'

When he had spoken these words, the venerable Vidura was insulted by Duryodhana whose lips trembled with rage, and who was accompanied by his own brothers, by Sakuni, and by Karna. Duryodhana said: 'Who sent for this deceitful person to come here? He is just the son of a servant girl who has lived here on our charity. Throw him out of our house at once, taking with him nothing but his breath!' Although he was afflicted by these cruel words, Vidura did not respond. He simply got up and walked from the

> palace, leaving his bow at the door. He felt no anguish at what had happened, for he could understand that this is simply the way of the world.

The lesson imparted in this short passage from the Bhagavata is a relatively simple one. Many will already be familiar with the background story, which is taken from the Mahabharata, but the main point to note is Vidura's response to the horrible situation in which he finds himself. Although he is one of the elders of the family, he is insulted, belittled, and humiliated by the harsh words of his nephew Duryodhana. And yet he is able to tolerate this insult because of his higher knowledge of the world. He is aware that we all experience highs and lows in life, praise and insults, but that this is the nature of existence, and because of this philosophical outlook, he developed a sense of spiritual well-being. On this basis he is able to tolerate misfortune with a sense of equanimity, and thereby transcend the pain in his life.

The second episode is found in Chapter 8 of the Bhagavata's fourth book. This section tells the famous narrative of the child-saint Dhruva, who – like Vidura in the first passage – suffers insult and rejection. In Dhruva's case it is his father and step-mother who reject Dhruva; this is so traumatic that it spurs the child to leave home and seek solace in rigorous meditation practice in the jungle. In the extract below, the forest-bound Dhruva meets the sage Narada.

> Dhruva then began to practise a fierce form of yoga in order to redress the wrongs that had been done to him. On hearing what was occurring, the saintly Narada then came to the forest where Dhruva had made his abode, and touched him gently on the head. Marvelling at the spirit of the royal order, Narada then began to speak to Dhruva.
>
> 'How can you be feeling such a sense of disgrace when you are still but a child? Dissatisfaction

such as you are feeling can only arise from intense attachment to this world. You must understand that nothing can take place unless God wills it to be so, and so you should be satisfied with whatever fortune is bestowed upon you. You are now seeking the grace of God in order to reverse your ill fortune, but this is very difficult to achieve, and all but impossible for a child. Even renowned ascetics who practise the most austere forms of yoga take many lifetimes to achieve their goal, so give up these efforts you are making and wait until you older.

'When destiny brings pleasure in life, you should see it as the result of past righteous deeds, and in the same way, when destiny brings suffering, you must see it as the result of acts of wickedness performed in the past. Only by thinking in this way can you find satisfaction in life, and start out on the path to liberation. You should show love for those who are righteous, show kindness to those who are less well off than yourself, and show friendship towards all who are your equals. It is by acting in this way that you can escape from the grief you feel.'

On hearing these wise words of instruction, Dhruva replied to Narada, 'My lord, it is certainly true that persons like myself will find it very hard to follow the path of tranquillity you have spoken of. Anyone who does so will then transcend both happiness and pain. But I was born as a Kshatriya, a member of royal order, and cannot see the world with such an equal disposition. My heart has been broken by the harsh words of my stepmother, Suruchi, and so your words of wisdom do not appeal to me. I have resolved to achieve a position of power, such as was never gained by any of my ancestors, so you please tell me how I can achieve such a position.'

> Narada then accepted Dhruva's submission, and initiated him with the sacred mantra *om namo bhagavate vasudevaya*. After meditating on this mantra for many years, Sri Vishnu himself appeared to Dhruva and blessed him with the gifts he sought. Empowered in this way, Dhruva returned to his home and was then able to recover his position of prominence in the kingdom, of which his step-mother had sought to deprive him.

This excerpt provides a counterpoint to the example of Vidura in the first passage. Whereas Vidura had already developed a sense of spiritual well-being, and could thus transcend his pain, here we read of Dhruva respectfully and honestly acknowledging that he is unable to accept his counsellor's advice. 'My heart has been pierced,' he effectively says, 'and thus your advice to transcend it, as wise and true as it may be, won't work for me. I need to heal these wounds first.' This admission is striking and gives us a wonderful example of Hinduism's teaching that one must approach spirituality with honesty and awareness of where one is at. Equally praise-worthy is Narada's broadmindedness and non-attachment as one in the role of a caregiver; he hears Dhruva, changes course, and recommends practical steps for Dhruva to take to come to spiritual realisation himself. The larger narrative ultimately offers a transcendent resolution to Dhruva's conflict; it is still important to note, however, that this resolution comes about after Dhruva acknowledges and owns his pain.

Together, the two episodes suggest two approaches – or perhaps two facets of one integrated approach – to caring for one's spiritual well-being. On the one hand, a Hindu chaplain can and should draw on spiritual practices and scriptural guidance to connect those in need with a higher reality. On the other, chaplains must be careful to approach people as they really are and be sensitive to their immediate emotional needs, and not simply point them toward an ideal. This is especially so in cases where there may be deeper underlying issues of mental or emotional instability; spiritual practice or prayer regiments must not be presented as substitutes for needed medical treatment or psychological counselling.

SUFFERING, LOSS, AND GRIEF

Related to spiritual well-being is the care that chaplains can provide to those coping with tragedy, loss, or bereavement. In some ways, this care may be seen as a specific application of caring for spiritual well-being. We include it as a separate section here, however, because it calls on chaplains to apply particular skills and employ particular sensitivities. Indeed, there is a balance to be struck between natural compassion for any person who is suffering in this way, and a more rational, philosophical discussion of the nature of human existence. Both of these can be immensely comforting, and when taken together provide a vital form of support, but must be exercised with thoughtfulness and maturity.

Here, we might employ an oft-cited tripartite schema for looking at broad categories of Hindu responses to grief counselling: approaches that emphasise the philosophical dimension (*jnana*), the ritual dimension (*karma*), and the devotional dimension (*bhakti*). Of course, we do not mean to suggest that such classifications are rigid and mutually exclusive categories; rather, as we have already seen, in practice they often overlap and even conflate into one another. Still, we use them here as a tool to examine resources available to the Hindu chaplain.

Perhaps the most obvious approach to grief counselling, and often the first one Hindu religious leaders turn to – although it is open to debate as to whether it ought to be – is the offering of metaphysical insights into the nature of life and death. The Hindu tradition has numerous resources to offer in this respect, especially with regard to scriptural texts like the Upanishads and the Bhagavad-gita. Many Hindus, for instance, turn to the story of Nachiketa – a philosophical treatise on death in the form of a narrative – found in the Katha Upanishad. Even more popular among contemporary Hindus, perhaps, is the Bhagavad-gita, and in particular its exposition on the eternality of the soul, the *atman*. In Chapter 2 of the Gita, as Krishna's first response to Arjuna's dilemma, we find a discourse on the eternal nature of the *atman*, and on the cycle of rebirth as dictated by the force of karma, past actions (2.11–27). This is a very useful passage to refer to and the chaplain would be well advised to study it carefully. Here are a few examples of its teachings:

dehino 'smin yatha dehe
kaumaram yauvanam jara
tatha dehantara-praptir
dhiras tatra na muhyati

> As this embodied soul, passes within the body from childhood, to youth, to old age, so it also passes on to another bodily form. The wise one is not confounded by such a process (Bhagavad-gita 2.13)

vasamsi jirnani yatha vihaya
navani grihnati naro 'parani
tatha sharirani vihaya jirnany
anyani samyati navani dehi

> A man casts off old clothes and puts on others that are new. In just the same way, the soul casts off its old body and then accepts another new form. (Bhagavad-gita 2.22)

jatasya hi dhruvo mrityur
dhruvam janma mritasya cha
tasmad apariharye 'rthe
na tvam sochitum arhasi

> For one who is born death is a certainty, and for one who has died rebirth is certain. Therefore you must not grieve over that which is unavoidable. (Bhagavad-gita 2.27)

matra-sparsas tu kaunteya
sitoshna-sukha-duhkha-dah
agamapayino 'nityas
tams titikshasva bharata

> Winter and summer, joy and distress, are simply perceptions of the senses, Kaunteya. They come and they go; they are never permanent. Therefore you should learn to tolerate them, Bharata. (Bhagavad-gita 2.14)

The higher understanding of life and death offered by Hindu teachings is also an important source of comfort as they reveal that death is not the end of an individual's existence. These teachings also urge us towards a more philosophical and detached view of life, an understanding that despite all the joys of life, suffering is also an inevitable part of existence, and can only be transcended by cultivating a higher vision of the world. From even our cursory glance at such references, however, a challenge becomes glaringly obvious. One can see how the philosophical perspective, while noble and rational in the abstract sense, can appear to be cold, and perhaps even heartless, when applied. Here, it is vitally important that the chaplain temper such teachings with other teachings – and personal actions and gestures – evincing genuine concern and compassion. He or she would be well advised to draw from scriptural statements endorsing the idea that we soothe, rather than dismiss or negate, the suffering of others. For instance, in the Bhagavad-gita, Krishna teaches:

yo mam pasyati
sarvam cha mayi pasyati
tasyaham na pranasyami
sa cha me na pranasyati

sarva-bhuta-sthitam yo mam
bhajaty ekatvam asthitah
sarvatha vartamano 'pi
so yogi mayi vartate

atmaupamyena sarvatra
samam pasyati yo 'rjuna
sukham va yadi va duhkham
so yogi paramo matah

> For one who sees me everywhere, and who sees everything as existing within me, I am never lost and nor is he ever lost to me.
>
> Whatever his way of life may be, one who adheres to this sense of oneness and worships me as being situated within all beings is a practitioner of yoga (yogin) who exists in me.
>
> One who sees everything in relation to his own self, Arjuna, and thus regards pleasure and suffering with equanimity, is considered to be the highest practitioner of yoga. (Bhagavad-gita 6.30–32)

This is an especially relevant passage, both for those coping with grief and those administering care. Krishna re-assures us that he is never lost to us, and is present with us even in our time of grief or pain. Perhaps most striking of all, Krishna defines one who is most advanced in yoga practice in terms of his or her capacity to experience empathy and compassion for others. One striving toward the ideals of the Gita, therefore, must do so in a spirit of compassion and kinship with others – both in their celebrations and in their grief. Where we speak of such compassion we are back in the realm of dharma, for as we have discussed, to do whatever is possible to alleviate the suffering of others is a key element in our understanding of the nature of dharma. Those who are grieving will often have numerous day-to-day concerns to be dealt with, and providing help with these can be a very significant form of assistance. Moreover, just to spend time with grieving persons, to listen to them, and to try in some way to share their distress can bring comfort, especially when combined with religious and philosophical explanations of the travails of life on earth. The philosophical perspective is certainly important but when taken alone it can appear cold and dispassionate, and a chaplain must take care to combine the religious teachings with empathy and compassion, the true essence of dharma.

A related caution: a chaplain might also seek to refer to the concept of karma to provide some explanation for the suffering a person is undergoing. While there is certainly philosophical justification for this, a high degree of caution is called for. Simply to assert that a person's grief and misery is the result of past actions can be dismissive and callous at best, and a serious and damaging misappropriation of the complex doctrine of karma, at worst. Again, any such discussion must be tempered by words and actions of empathy and comfort.

Of course, another definition of karma in the Hindu worldview is religious or ritual action, and this too is an approach Hindu traditions take to helping people cope with grief. Hindus enact a number of rituals following the death of a family member. Chaplains who are also trained as Hindu ritual priests can especially play an important role here. While it will not usually be the role of non-priest chaplains to officiate over such rituals, for that is generally the domain of the Hindu priesthood, all Hindu chaplains might still find meaningful ways to help family members to cope with their loss. The chaplain can provide further comfort by properly explaining the rituals and helping family members to connect with them in a personal way. He or she can also offer solace to family members by helping them see the ritual as a way to benefit and honour the deceased loved one in the afterlife. Hindu texts are clear that offerings made in the *shraddha* ceremony performed by the priest become a source of joy and prosperity for the recipient. We also learn from the Mahabharata that gifts of charity made on behalf of the deceased have a similar effect. This was undertaken by Dhritarashtra on behalf of his sons, slain in the great conflict at Kurukshetra, though the funds for such gifts were provided by the magnanimous Yudhishthira. The chaplain can help family members to find innovative ways to continue this tradition in relevant contemporary settings. In the process, he or she can also find appropriate opportunities to engage the family members in conversations about the deceased and help them to process their grief.

One chaplain had this experience in offering spiritual care to a family whose father passed away after a prolonged battle with cancer:

> At first the family informed me that they were not in need of (or interested in) any kind of grief counselling, but enlisted my help in performing and explaining some of the rituals associated with the last rites. Over the course of the few days that we worked together on these arrangements, we grew closer and the family members began to open up about their feelings and the challenges they faced in trying to cope with the death of their father and husband. Together, we used the various rituals and scripture readings as ways of talking about and working through what they were feeling.

As we have discussed, despite the focus Hindu traditions give to religious philosophy and ritual action, most practising Hindus are drawn primarily to its theistic and devotional forms. For these Hindus, faith in metaphysics and ritual observance is intertwined with – and sometimes even revolves around – a profound belief in the presence and the grace of God. As we have seen, most Hindus living in the Western world display devotion to Krishna, Rama, Shiva, and Devi and many will find comfort in such devotion in times of sorrow. Thus, the third approach which a chaplain might employ in offering comfort is the devotional one. At times of distress, the world can seem empty, and we may feel lost and devoid of comfort and protection. If the chaplain can seek to emphasise the belief in the higher oversight of a loving deity then this may bring comfort to a grieving person, particularly when his or her words are supported by the words of God found in Hindu texts. Here, the chaplain might evoke Hinduism's vision of the worshipper as the child or dependent of the deity to help the family members cope with their loss by looking to God in their time of distress. Many times over in Hindu texts, these deities express their love and commitment towards those who are devoted to them and promise to provide their devotees with grace, blessings, and comfort. Moreover, these texts emphasise God's role as the absolute controller of the world and implore the worshipper to see everything that happens as being, in some way, a manifestation of his will and expression of his concern. The devotional approach suggests, in a sense, that God's grace can be found even in the midst of loss. Again we can find such assurance within the verses of the Bhagavad-gita:

yo mam pasyati sarvatra
sarvam cha mayi pasyati
tasyaham na pranasyami
sa cha me na pranasyati

> For one who sees me everywhere, and who sees everything as existing within me, I am never lost and nor is he ever lost to me. (Bhagavad-gita 6.30)

This is an especially significant statement, for at least two reasons. First, this verse underscores a core teaching on the presence of the divine in everything (although, as we have discussed, various schools of Hindu philosophy have differed in how we might understand this omnipresence). Secondly, and more germane to our discussion, the verse implies that seeing God in everything – arguably even in the pain of grieving – can awaken an awareness that transcends loss. A chaplain can draw from these words to bring comfort to a distressed or grieving person. The same idea is echoed, and expressed even more fervently, in devotional texts such as Ramcharitmanas, Shiva Purana, Devi-Bhagavata Purana, and the Bhagavata Purana. For instance, remarkable and moving expressions of divine love can be found in Tulsidas's Ramcharitmanas; the Hindu chaplain might refer to this text, or invite the family member to read passages, as a way of providing comfort and reflecting on the absolute grace of God.

In one university chaplain's experience:

> A few years ago, I had occasion to offer care to two young ladies – twin sisters, both students at the university – who were grieving the loss of a favourite aunt to cancer. This marked the sisters' first experience with the death of a close family member, and both struggled to cope with it. As we explored various approaches together, one of the girls mentioned that the aunt was particularly fond of chanting the Hanuman Chalisa, a famous devotional song in praise of the deity Hanuman who is celebrated as an exemplar of devotion, courage, and strength. I suggested that we recite the prayer together as a way of honouring their aunt and seeking Hanuman's blessings for her. Chanting together was a powerful and moving experience; afterwards, they reflected on how it helped them to say goodbye to their aunt. One sister felt that the prayer

> assured her that Hanuman was with them, protecting the aunt's soul and comforting the family in their sadness. The other sister saw the experience more in terms of a way to invoke memories of the aunt and thus stay connected with her in spirit. The experience reminded me that, beyond their explicit function of connecting us with God, devotional texts may also help to bring worshippers closer to their departed loved ones and to one another.

In this section we have looked only briefly at the three broad categories of a Hindu approach to grief counselling, loosely corresponding to emphases on *jnana*, *karma*, and *bhakti.* Hindu chaplains will likely utilise all of these to varying extents, and must discern how best to do so in light of the situation at hand and the inclinations of the grieving person. The choice of particular text or practice will vary based on a number of factors and the chaplain must be sensitive to these. Here again, the importance of listening over speaking is brought to the fore.

PUNISHMENT, DETENTION, AND FREEDOM

A third context in which Hindu chaplains might be called on to give spiritual care involves punishment and detention – prison for example.

While our discussion so far would also be relevant here, we should also consider two additional facets more particular to this context. First, the chaplain may be called on to navigate issues of fairness, guilt, innocence, justice, and mercy. Secondly, chaplains in this context might also be given opportunities to help detainees reflect upon the spiritual dimensions to concepts such as freedom and choice.

Based on our previous discussion of Hinduism's emphasis on not harming and absolute compassion, one might assume that the idea of punishment would be entirely antithetical to Sanatana Dharma. This would be an incomplete understanding. Alongside the concern and compassion expressed for others, the teachings on dharma are also vitally concerned with the need for social order, as it is only in such a context that universal well-being can prevail. The teachings of the Hindu tradition often reveal the tension that can arise between the need for social order and universal compassion. This tension is particularly apparent within the narrative of the Mahabharata, where Yudhishthira constantly urges forgiveness and restraint whilst his brothers (and even Krishna) insist that wrongdoers must be punished for their misdeeds. Here is a passage from the Mahabharata that nicely illustrates the tension we have highlighted and one of the ways in which it can be resolved.

> Yudhishthira asked: 'Tell me, grandfather, how is it possible for a king to protect his subjects without harming anyone?'
>
> Bhishma said: 'In this connection they narrate this ancient account of a conversation that took place between King Dyumatsena and his son, Satyavan. When a number of criminals were brought before Dyumatsena for punishment, Satyavan spoke the following words to him. "Sometimes dharma takes the form of wickedness, and wickedness takes the form of dharma, but it can never be possible that the harming of individuals in this way is in accordance with dharma."'
>
> Dyumatsena said: 'If the sparing of those who deserve punishment be accepted, Satyavan, then all distinction between righteousness and wrongdoing would vanish and no one would respect the property of another. If wrongdoers are not punished then how can society continue? If you know the answer to this question, then tell me.'
>
> Satyavan said: 'It is true that if a person commits a crime he must be punished, but that punishment

should not be harsh and should not harm the body of the offender. If the punishment be too harsh, many others will suffer as well, including the wife, children, and parents of the offender. Therefore the king must think very carefully about the nature of the punishment to be ordained.

'Sometimes wicked people can be influenced by those who are good and can change their behaviour, and sometimes good children are born from those who are wicked. Therefore a gentle form of punishment is most appropriate. This should be done by means of fines or perhaps limited periods of imprisonment, but their relatives should never be made to suffer alongside them. If they swear in front of a worthy brahmin never to commit such acts again, then they should be discharged without punishment. But those who offend repeatedly should not be treated in this way and must undergo some form of punishment. Only those who commit a first offence should be dismissed without punishment.'

Dyumatsena said: 'As long as a person does not breach the injunctions of the law, he may be regarded as one who is righteous. But if those who break the law are not punished then the whole notion of law becomes meaningless. In ancient times people were more righteous than today and they could be governed simply by words of correction. But today robbers and wrongdoers cannot be restrained in this gentle way. The robber has no respect for society and will steal from anyone, even from a corpse, so who would respect any promise they might make to reform their conduct?'

Satyavan said: 'When there are many thieves and robbers active in a kingdom, the rulers become

> ashamed and sacrifice their own lives to ensure the welfare of their subjects who are oppressed by miscreants. People will behave properly only when there is fear of the law but rulers should never punish wrongdoers simply to gain revenge.
>
> 'A ruler who just seeks his own pleasure and yet endeavours to restrain others becomes an object of contempt. If a person commits offences he must be restrained by the ruler in order to prevent him from committing further offences, and harming the honest citizens. But the rulers must ensure that their own conduct is proper before they can seek to impose sanction on others.
>
> 'My grandfather was the kindest of men and out of pity for others always adhered to the dharma of ahimsa. He once said to me, "In previous ages when people were naturally righteous there was no need for rulers to inflict punishment. But in the present age, if a king attempts to rule on the basis of ahimsa, confusion and chaos will be the result, and the king must then resort to various forms of punishment in order to restrain the wrongdoers."'
>
> (Mahabharata, Book 12, Chapter 259)

The passage attempts to reconcile the precepts of compassion and ahimsa, central to Sanatana Dharma, with the necessity of maintaining law and order within a state so that citizens can flourish and live happily. The text suggests that punishment can be reconciled with compassion if it is administered by a ruler motivated by concern for the welfare of others; it is never to be an act of pure vengeance or performed on the basis of anger and hatred. A similar idea is encountered in the Bhagavad-gita where Krishna urges Arjuna to confront the wrongdoers, not out of any sense of vengeance or anger, but because to do so is his duty and will be of benefit to the whole of society. In the third chapter he makes this point quite clear:

karmanaiva hi samsiddhim
asthita janakadayah
loka-samgraham evapi
sampasyan kartum arhasi

> It is was through action alone that kings of the past such as Janaka achieved perfection. Now, thinking only of the welfare of the world, you must engage in this warlike action. (Bhagavad-gita 3.20)

Here the key phrase is *loka-samgraham*, meaning the welfare of the world; according to Krishna's teachings, the welfare of others should be Arjuna's only motivation in acting aggressively against the wrongdoers who confront him.

Hindu chaplains ministering to detainees – and sometimes also to those tasked with administering punishment, such as prison wardens – will have to constantly engage with this tension. At the same time, prison can be an extremely harsh environment, especially for first-time offenders, and persons undergoing punishment of this type will often need support from the chaplain in order to get through their ordeal.

Detainees often experience feelings of guilt or regret; others may feel anger or see themselves as being unjustly targeted. Some see prison as an opportunity to rectify themselves, while others sink into a sense of despair or feel rejected. A prisoner may experience all of these emotions and fluctuate in his or her attitude from day to day. The chaplain must address all these needs, and help the detainee to find spiritual meaning in the midst of their punishment. A chaplain might reference the concept of dharma, as we have already discussed, and in particular the emphasis we find on ensuring that our actions and words cause no harm to others, and that we are as honest as possible in all our dealings. In this way, the chaplain can help the detainee to bring his or her behaviour and actions into line with dharmic principles.

It is not appropriate for a chaplain to concern him or herself with judging the innocence or guilt of the prisoner. In fact, as a general rule, a chaplain should only do so when the detainee brings this topic up. Even then, the chaplain must be sensitive to the detainee's feelings and allow him or her to steer the conversation. The chaplain's task is to offer care, not to re-adjudicate the prisoner's case or become a legal advocate on his or her behalf.

There are other ways for the chaplain to advocate for prisoners – in particular, in matters related to their spiritual or religious needs. For instance, many Hindus adhere to a vegetarian diet (and some have more restrictive dietary needs beyond this, such as abstaining from onions and garlic). The chaplain can play an essential role in advocating for the prisoner to receive such meals and in helping the rest of the prison administration to better understand the religious significance. The chaplain may also advocate for prisoners to be given time to engage in religious practice (such as meditation, yoga, or *jap* chanting) or have access to religious books, prayer beads, or the accoutrements of puja (ritual worship). Of course, prisons have their own policies and regulations, and must balance these with the need to accommodate prisoners' legitimate religious needs. The chaplain can be a critical partner in this process.

A second way in which chaplains might offer care in a prison would be to help prisoners to see their detainment as an opportunity to reflect on the deeper meaning of freedom. In the most literal sense, prisoners are deprived of their freedom; they are confined and compelled to conform to the strictures of the prison. But from a Hindu perspective, freedom also means freedom of the mind, and this freedom can be achieved in any physical circumstance. Moreover, the question may be raised as to the extent to which any person living in the world is actually free, as responsibilities and desires will often force us to follow a course of action that is unwelcome and unwanted.

Hindu teachings assert that true freedom is always inhibited by materialistic desires, which compel us to act in ways that are arduous and sometimes immoral. In the Bhagavad-gita, Arjuna asks why it is that persons act in sinful ways; the response from Krishna is unequivocal:

arjuna uvacha
atha kena prayukto 'yam
papam charati purushah
anicchan api varshneya
balad iva niyojitah

> Arjuna said: What is it that makes a person act in sinful ways even when he has no real desire to do so. It is as if he is compelled by some external force to act in this way. (Bhagavad-gita 3.36)

sri bhagavan uvacha
kama esha krodha esha
rajo-guna-samudbhavah
mahashano maha-papma
viddhy enam iha vairinam

> The Lord said: It is desire and it is anger, which arise from the quality known as *rajas*. It is like a blazing fire and is the source of all wickedness; you should know that this is the real enemy. (Bhagavad-gita 3.37)

Here Arjuna makes an interesting point, and the response from Krishna is equally insightful. One may not wish to act in an immoral or criminal manner but it seems that at times one is almost compelled to do so, as if being acted upon by some external force. What is this force? It is the blazing desires we have, or it may be the anger we are subject to when desires are frustrated. So in this sense we might conclude that real freedom comes only insofar as one is able to transcend desire, and this applies equally to those who are free to live in society and to those who have been incarcerated. In either situation, Hindu texts explain, our real prison cell is an internal one and real freedom is only achieved through spiritual practice. The chaplain can draw from these teachings to encourage detainees to approach their situation in a new way and to challenge conventional notions of freedom and bondage. A chaplain describes this very situation:

> I am serving as a chaplain to a young Hindu man who is in prison awaiting trial. It is his first time being in any sort of trouble with the law, and he claims that he has been wrongly imprisoned as a case of mistaken identity. When he was first incarcerated, he experienced shock, depression, and feelings of anger and despair. However, as he turned toward prayer and spiritual practices such as meditation and reading from the Bhagavad-gita, his perspective began to change. He described experiencing feelings of gratitude as he re-focused on his relationship with God. He told me how before this experience, he had put his faith on the back-burner. Although hailing from a very observant Hindu family and having grown up attending temples and Hindu summer camps regularly, as a young adult he found himself placing more energy into his high-pressure work, building and maintaining a materially lavish lifestyle, and pursuing romantic relationships. In prison, he shared with me, he was brought face to face with how superficial and hollow his lifestyle had become. Suddenly stripped of all of those distractions, he could dive into his spiritual exploration with new sense of appreciation of its value. Fittingly, he now describes this time in prison as having 'opened the door' for him and being a time of 'real freedom'. We now hold weekly phone

> meetings in which we read relevant excerpts from Hindu texts together and discuss their application to his situation.

As this anecdote shows, prison can be an opportunity for those who are detained to broaden their horizons through study, contemplation, or meditation. Chaplains can be of real assistance here. Practically, chaplains can supply Hindu books – which are generally hard to come by in prisons – and encourage prisoners to consider life more deeply. The chaplain can also be available as a study partner or discussion partner for prisoners interested in reading texts like the Bhagavad-gita or Upanishads. As always, the chaplain should avoid dogmatic assertions or proselytising, and must conduct conversations in an open and encouraging manner.

Another way a Hindu chaplain can care for those in prison might be to offer prisoners (Hindu and non-Hindu alike) sessions of meditation and yoga; a Hindu chaplain could teach the basic techniques informally or even conduct classes. We have discussed some simple techniques already, and these can be adapted to this context. Again, a chaplain would have to work with the relevant authorities to ensure that any such efforts do not conflict with policy or regulations. For instance, the use of prayer beads or yoga mats may require special approval. Chaplain-facilitated meditation and yoga may not be possible in all prisons, but where authorities are open to the suggestion and happy to provide the necessary space and facilities, Hindu chaplains can help provide this service.

As we have seen, despite its emphasis on not harming and compassion, the spirit of Sanatana Dharma does not preclude the idea of punishment. Rather, authorities should act vigorously for the suppression of crime and upholding law, motivated by a spirit of compassion for all. As the Bhagavad-gita makes clear, the inflicting of punishment should never be done out of anger, vengeance, or malice, but because it is necessary for the greater good of society as a whole. Moreover, those who are imprisoned should be treated with kindness and respect, their rights and needs should be honoured, and every attempt should be made to help them to achieve reform and rehabilitation. The Hindu chaplain can play a role in this, and may help those imprisoned find spiritual meaning – and even a sense of freedom and contentment – in their situation.

VIOLENCE AND MILITARY DEFENCE

The tension between compassion and justice that we referenced in the last section is also at the heart of the final context we will examine in this section – that of state-sanctioned violence and military defence. How might a Hindu chaplain offer spiritual care here? In addition to the ways we have already discussed, chaplains can also offer care to Hindus in the military in two specific ways: by helping them to reconcile their faith with the violent nature of military service, and by helping them to balance their commitments to the larger unit with their individual needs for self-care.

First, we must explore the complex ways the tradition negotiates the role of violence. On the one hand, Hinduism seems to favour non-violence. We have already emphasised the salience of ahimsa as a dominant characteristic of Sanatana Dharma. On the other hand, however, Hindu texts constantly reference violence and warfare. The great epics, the Mahabharata and the Ramayana, apparently champion military action against the forces of *adharma*. And perhaps most relevant to contemporary popular Hinduism, the Bhagavad-gita, is set on a battlefield and has Krishna urging Arjuna to warfare, even as he extols the virtue of ahimsa! What are Hindus to make of this apparent paradox?

A number of teachers and Hindu leaders have attempted to resolve the paradox; perhaps the best-known in recent history is Mahatma Gandhi. Gandhi referred to his beliefs as the 'religion of non-violence' but at the same time he declared himself to be a devoted follower of the Bhagavad-gita. Gandhi was well aware of this apparent paradox and sought to resolve it in two ways. Firstly, he suggested that the battlefield setting for the Bhagavad-gita should be taken metaphorically rather than literally, and that it should be understood as the conflict between the lower and higher forms of consciousness that exist in every person. Secondly, Gandhi pointed out that the main teaching of the Gita is that we should abandon all sense of selfish desire and act only out of duty or in service to others. Acts of violence, he contended, are almost always performed on the basis of desire and anger, and hence the desireless person, the Gita's ideal, will also naturally be non-violent.

Gandhi's attempt to free the Gita of its violent context by interpreting it as metaphor resonates with many readers. Indeed, re-visioning the Gita's setting as a symbolic rather than a literal battlefield has become quite popular in the modern era. Still, it is not without its problems. The Gita is part of the Mahabharata, a larger text steeped in martial and political affairs and which explicitly recognises the role of the military. Nor is the Gita the only scripture to pair spirituality and violence. Other Hindu texts – including the popular Puranas and the Ramayana – also frequently depict, and seemingly endorse, some violence. Moreover, none of the classical commentaries to these texts suggest that readers take them as allegory. Even today most Hindus seem to accept the events described in texts like the Gita to be, on some level at least, historical truth.

For our current discussion, Gandhi's second idea warrants more careful consideration. By pointing out that acts of violence are almost always motivated by desire and anger, Gandhi was able to draw an intimate connection between the ideals of desirelessness and non-violence. For Gandhi, violence and warfare represent the ultimate degradation of the human spirit, and hence ahimsa is both the means of achieving spiritual progress and the essential mark of one who is spiritually enlightened. As we have seen, dharma is frequently equated with ahimsa in the ancient texts, and there is no doubt that non-violence and not harming form a vital part of the Hindu revelation. Moreover, this assertion that violence generally arises from desire for personal or national gain is well attested, both from history and from the world we can observe around us.

However, Hindu teachings do not generally articulate Gandhi's form of absolute pacifism; rather, they invite us to consider alternative perspectives and negotiate the tensions around the use of violence to preserve the well-being of society. The Mahabharata, for instance, explores the tension between the pure virtue of non-violence and the necessity of using violence in considerable detail, with significant arguments coming from both sides. Here is what the peaceable Yudhishthira has to say on the subject:

> In all circumstances war is a sin. If you strike another person in battle, you are really striking yourself, and if you are struck down then victory and defeat are the same. Victory is not much different from defeat for even if a victorious king is not killed himself, many of his friends and loved ones will die in battle. Those who are quiet, modest, and virtuous, are often killed in battle whilst the wicked escape with their lives. Even after one's enemies have been slain then one's heart will be wracked by guilt and remorse for the suffering caused. Then if any of the enemy survive a defeat they will surely try to gather new forces to fight again so that the violence will continue. Victory creates animosity amongst surviving enemies whilst defeat brings nothing but sorrow.
>
> One who is peaceful can sleep happily with no worries over victory or defeat whilst the warlike person is always oppressed by fear and anxiety over what the future will bring. One who exterminates

> all his foes does not become renowned for greatness but is rather seen as being cruel and infamous. Enmity is never nullified by enmity but only grows stronger, like a fire fed by ghee. Hence there can be no peace without one party completely annihilating the other for those who have been defeated will always seek to continue the conflict by restoring their strength. The complete annihilation of the enemy may bring success but the cruelty of such an act can never be approved of.
>
> However, peace gained by giving up one's kingdom is almost as bad as death itself for it brings one to a state of utter ruin. We do not wish to give up our kingdom but neither do we want to see the extinction of our whole family. Therefore even if peace is accompanied by humiliation that will be the better course than taking up arms to fight. When all attempts at reconciliation fail then the time for war has come; when conciliation fails then frightful consequences follow. Learned men have seen the same thing in fights between dogs. First there is the wagging of the tail, then barking, then walking round each other, then showing teeth, then loud shouts, and finally fighting. In such a conflict, the stronger dog defeats the weaker and takes away its food. There is no difference with men; those who are powerful must never seek disputes to take away the property of the weak. (Mahabharata, Book 5, Chapter 70).

Yudhishthira, like Gandhi, offers an impassioned criticism of any recourse to violent means, arguing that violence destroys our humanity and is linked to the desire to seize another's property. Moreover, Yudhisthira suggests, violence will never truly settle a conflict, for when the defeated party regains its strength then the conflict will be renewed in an almost endless cycle. And yet this is not the final word when it comes to Hinduism's views on violence. We also find in Hindu teachings the advocacy of a form of dharma known as Kshatriya Dharma, which insists that it is the religious duty of kings and warriors to use their martial prowess in the protection of the weak. The Bhagavad-gita describes the qualities of such Kshatriyas:

shauryam tejo dhritir daksham
yuddhe chapy upalayanam
danam ishvara-bhavas cha
kshatram karma svabhava-jam

> Heroism, vigour, resolve, expertise, and never fleeing from battle, along with generosity and a lordly disposition; this is the set duty of the *kshatriya*, arising from his inherent nature. (Bhagavad-gita 18.43)

The Hindu tradition fully accepts the need for a class of highly trained and qualified personnel who will resort to violence – albeit measured and reasonable violence – when the need arises. Much more is said about the *kshatriya-dharma* in the Mahabharata, in Book 12 in particular. The epic repeatedly emphasises that without the *kshatriyas* society will collapse into a state of chaos and all people will suffer as a result. The text also specifies that such persons who have a duty to resort to military action must be highly trained not just in the science of warfare but in ethics and morality so that they do not abuse the power and responsibility invested in them.

In many ways, the Bhagavad-gita is an exploration of Hinduism's ambivalence around violence and warfare. Krishna's advice is essentially twofold. Arjuna must take up arms and fight in the battle; he is a *kshatriya* and it is his duty, his dharma, to stop the wrongdoers by acting against them militarily. Such acts of violence, however, must never be undertaken on the basis of selfish desire. It is a duty that must be performed for the welfare of society and not out of a longing for wealth or power.

While Hindu teachings recognise the necessity of recourse to violence to protect the well-being of society as a whole, they also offer some important caveats. Those designated to take on such a role must be persons of impeccable character who will never abuse the power and training they possess, and never use it with selfish intent. Moreover, acts of violence are to be undertaken only when the protection of the innocent provides just cause; hence warfare must never be an act of aggression based on imperialism or the expansion of national power. Again here, we might remember Krishna's instruction in the third chapter of the Bhagavad-gita to 'pursue this act of warfare, thinking only of the welfare of the world.' The key, it would seem, is the motive and consciousness with which one engages in necessary violence.

With this context as the framework, we can return to our discussion of how Hindu chaplains might offer care to Hindus in the military. Just as we have seen Hindu texts exhibit a degree of ambivalence about the role of state-sponsored violence, Hindu servicemen and women may also struggle to reconcile their faith with the violent nature of military service. Many might experience doubt – in themselves, in the correctness of their actions, or in their religious beliefs – and feelings of guilt. Others might turn their discomfort outward, evincing rage, vengeance, and a lack of self-control. Some may take the seemingly opposite route, embracing a superficial and misguided understanding of Hinduism's teachings on detachment to become emotionally withdrawn and apathetic. The Hindu chaplain can play a crucial role in helping in all of these situations by offering spiritual care and empathy, and by reminding them of the ideal of *kshatriya-dharma* – military engagement out of a sense of duty and in pursuance of the good of others, free from desire for gain or vengeance.

It is important that the chaplain emphasises that this is an ideal to aspire to and not a goal to be achieved overnight.

Chaplains must remind servicemen and women that Hindu texts present these ideals to encourage us to cultivate regular spiritual practices and strive toward them. Chaplain-organised scripture study, discussion groups, and meditation sessions may also be very helpful in this regard.

Here is one chaplain's experience:

> While I have not served as a military chaplain myself, I have had occasion to work with young Hindus who are returning from combat. One veteran, from a very religious Hindu family in the United States, relayed his experience to me. His parents were community leaders in his town; his father was one of the founders of their local Hindu temple and his mother was the main Sunday School teacher. When he enlisted, his family and others in the community were very supportive and constantly compared him to Arjuna. However, after his first tour of duty in Iraq, he began to feel a dissonance between his beliefs as a Hindu and his experience in war, accompanied by strong feelings of guilt, inadequacy, and frustration around his identity. The comparison to Arjuna became especially painful for him, and he became unable to even touch his copy of the Gita much less read it. With time, he began to heal – simple meditation and yoga practices were especially helpful.

This serves as a reminder to chaplains that each case is unique and that sometimes emphasising the ideal or pointing to scriptural examples may have adverse effects. As we have discussed, chaplains must be active listeners and remain flexible and sensitive to the needs of the individual in any given situation.

Some Hindus in the military rely on compartmentalisation as a coping mechanism. They behave like one person in the military setting and a different person in the context of family, temple community, or civilian life. This tendency can lead to feelings of being 'a divided self,' and take a heavy emotional and psychological toll on an individual.

Again, we can learn from a chaplain's experience:

> I served as a youth counsellor at a Hindu summer camp several years ago. One of my fellow counsellors was a young Hindu American veteran, recently returned from Afghanistan. As a gifted storyteller and charismatic teacher, he was easily the most popular counsellor at the camp – especially among the teenage boys who saw him as the epitome of the cool war hero. He enjoyed constantly joking around with the campers and shared inspiring stories with them. Unfortunately, one day a camper accidentally and innocently misplaced something belonging to him, and he snapped, screaming and cursing at the campers and punching a wall. Although he later apologised, the incident was traumatising for all involved. In speaking with him later, I learned that he privately struggled with PTSD, depression, and insomnia (among other emotional and physical ramifications of his time in combat), and that he had tried to keep those aspects of his life entirely separate from his work with the Hindu youth. As we spoke, I reflected on the dangers I saw in this approach and encouraged him to find ways to integrate the two sides of his life.

Another way that Hindu chaplains might help those in the military is by emphasising the need for self-care. The culture of the military tends to favour the collective over the individual – the needs of the unit, the service, or the nation generally come first. In this respect, military life bears some similarity to traditional Hindu culture, where the benefit to the larger group – the extended family, the temple group, the caste community – take precedence over one's personal needs. These can be noble ideals. At the same time, these ideals must be balanced with the need for appropriate self-care. The reality is that meeting individual needs is vital to the survival of the individual and the larger group. Here, Hindu chaplains have an important part to play. The chaplain can remind servicemen and women that in order to serve others effectively, they must be physically, emotionally, and spiritually healthy. Balance, moderation, and sustainability are key principles. For instance, the Bhagavad-gita espouses the idea that to be truly caring and empathic to others, one must be a yogi; yogis, the text informs us, are measured and balanced in their diet, rest, and recreation (6.17). The chaplain can use such references to help Hindus in the military see their service to others, their health and well-being, and their spiritual and religious commitments as part of the same continuum. Still, Hindus in the military in the West are a minority, and so they might feel awkward about requesting religious accommodation or expressing their needs. Chaplains might also fulfil a more practical role, helping military personnel obtain the resources needed to practice their faith and advocating on their behalf if necessary. For instance, a chaplain could help to provide copies of Hindu texts to servicemen and women, or advocate on their behalf to receive special vegetarian meals. In this regard, Hindu chaplains can take inspiration and practical guidance from their counterparts in the Muslim, Sikh, and Jewish faiths.

CONCLUSION

In this session, we examined Hindu perspectives on care and compassion, and explored how a Hindu chaplain might serve as a care-giver in a number of contexts. While each of these provides unique challenges and call for specific approaches, a common feature that emerges is that the chaplain serves to connect Hindus in contemporary settings with resources from the tradition.

In the next session we will continue to explore this idea while looking at a host of other roles that the Hindu chaplain must play in service to his or her community.

2. CHAPLAINCY ROLES

In the previous session, we looked at the chaplain as a giver of spiritual care. This role – what we might call the 'pastoral' role, to borrow terminology from Christian and Jewish traditions – is arguably at the heart of a chaplain's job. At the same time, to effectively serve his or her community a Hindu chaplain might have to play a number of other roles as well. In this session, we will look at four of these.

CHAPLAIN AS COUNSELLOR

As we have seen, the primary role of the chaplain is to provide comfort, support, advice, and guidance to members of his or her religious communities (and indeed to others when appropriate). In the first session, we explored how, in different contexts, Hindu chaplains could support Hindus in grief, stress, and emotional need. In addition to (and often in concert with) this type of support, the chaplain may find him- or herself called upon to explicitly give counsel. While this might represent a continuation of our discussion around spiritual care, here the focus is on the explicit giving of guidance and advice. 'What does my religion have to say about this situation that I find myself in?' a Hindu might ask, 'How, as a Hindu, might I approach this challenge I am faced with? How might my faith inform my action?'

Historically, and to some extent today, the role of counsellor in Hindu society was often fulfilled by the elders of the family and community who took responsibility for the good conduct and emotional well-being of those dependent upon them. In addition, the ancient texts also speak of providing guidance and support as one of the principal roles of the brahmins, who had access to and knowledge of the wisdom offered by the religious tradition as a whole. It would not be uncommon for individual communities or even families to have their own spiritual preceptors to whom they could turn to for help in applying the teachings of the tradition or scriptures to specific situations or challenges.

In modern societies, however, the situation has dramatically changed. Increasingly Hindus no longer live in close-knit rural communities, but in the complex social settings of the large cities. Living as a nuclear rather than extended family is increasingly the norm, caste identity is less significant than before, and brahmins have come to primarily play the role of ritual priests rather than spiritual and moral guides to their communities. Moreover, in many instances linguistic and cultural barriers prevent Hindus – especially younger Hindus who may not be fluent in Indian languages – to meaningfully converse with these priests.

Another traditional source for advice and counsel within Hindu traditions would be from individuals known as sadhus, persons deemed to be spiritually awakened or especially adept in their spiritual practice. Such 'holy men' or 'holy women' might also hold a position within a Hindu religious institution. The sadhu may or may not be a brahmin; generally, Hindus deem the spiritual power and purity the sadhu possesses to be most significant. The role played by the sadhu has its own limitations, however. For one thing, although they might be respected by all Hindus, sadhus are only likely to be seen as guides or confidantes within their specific lineages or sects. Thus, their impact is limited along sectarian lines. Secondly, it is debatable whether or not it is always appropriate for sadhus to give guidance to Hindus living and working in the world, or whether they are competent to do so. Since sadhus often live detached lives outside of mainstream society, some may feel that they cannot truly relate to the struggles and challenges of those within it.

It is in this new environment that the role of the chaplain emerges as being of particular significance, fulfilling many of the functions previously ascribed to community leaders, sadhus, and brahmins. There are numerous accounts in the ancient Sanskrit texts of how great leaders sought the advice of learned brahmins or holy men, and in some parts of India, or within some orthodox communities, brahmins and sadhus may still fulfil this role; in the modern context and especially in the Western world it is much less frequently the case.

What then of the Hindu chaplain? Clearly there is a need to revive the traditional function played by the brahmins but without the insistence that such guidance be given only by those of brahmin birth or who function as ritual priests. The essential qualifications required are skill in counselling and a wide ranging knowledge of the resources offered by the Hindu tradition, along with an understanding of the best ways in which these resources might be used. Here we must emphasise that the chaplain need not 'know' Hinduism's response to every situation (if such a thing were even possible), he or she need only know of the resources and how such resources might be drawn upon. By acquiring these essential skills, the chaplain may come to fulfil the need left vacant by family elders, or take on the role largely given up by the brahmin priests and for which the traditional sadhus are often ill-equipped. In socially and economically modernised societies this new role emerges, and it is our job here to work out how it can best be fulfilled by the Hindu chaplain.

In trying to articulate a Hindu model of chaplaincy we must also acknowledge that we are analogising, and drawing from, other religious traditions and even secular models. For instance, the institutional forms that Christianity has adopted lend themselves to the vocation of chaplaincy. Within the Hindu tradition, however, it seems to be a matter of creating a new role from the resources available to us. This can combine skills learned from Christian and other chaplains, training in modern forms of counselling, and most especially learning to make use of the wisdom of the Hindu tradition by amalgamating and harmonising it with those counselling skills. This might appear to be a daunting task, but we can take encouragement from the fact that throughout its history Hinduism has always developed, grown, and adapted to meet the needs of its communities in changing social and economic environments. It is what Hinduism does, and there is no doubt that it will do so again in the contemporary world. We need not approach chaplaincy as a 'foreign' creation, then, but as part of the dynamic process of evolution of Hinduism and Hindu communities.

Another interesting and encouraging factor to note is that modern counselling techniques very often echo or find resonance with the wisdom espoused by Hindu texts. A number of thinkers have held up the Bhagavad-gita, for example, as a perfect counselling session in which Krishna directly addresses Arjuna's grief and thereby relieves him from the stress he is under. Krishna's message of detachment is one that still has significance today, and is one the chaplain can make use of. At the same time, there are many contemporary counselling techniques that a chaplain might also learn from and draw upon to supplement Hindu wisdom.

As we have seen, Hindu chaplains looking to articulate Hindu dharma will likely find themselves engaging with the tradition's emphasis on compassion, honesty, concern for others, and not harming. There are numerous accounts in Hindu texts that highlight these qualities, and the chaplain can make use of these in discussing situations or issues with those he or she is counselling.

There are two pitfalls that Hindu chaplains taking on the role of counsellors should guard against.

First, they would be advised to avoid identifying too strongly with a position of religious authority. In this respect, the role demands that the approach taken by a chaplain be somewhat different from that of the brahmins or sadhus who will speak from a position of authority and often present themselves as experts on Hindu doctrine. By contrast, the chaplain's 'expertise' as a counsellor will be found more in his or her willingness to help those he or she is counselling by being present, actively listening, and connecting others with resources from within and outside of Hindu teachings.

Secondly, the Hindu chaplain should guard against the tendency to conflate ministry (i.e. offering presence, comfort, and guidance) and missionising (i.e. preaching and proselytising). The chaplain should not be a preacher but a friend, a comforter, and a helper in times of need. He or she should listen carefully to the words of others and use their skill and resources in the most appropriate way. As far as possible, the Hindu chaplain should leave the other parties to reach their own conclusions. Hindu chaplains may be most comfortable with, and even draw most from, the traditions they are familiar with or inspired by. This is not a problem per se, but chaplains must ensure that they are not pushing a sectarian agenda in the guise of counselling. A chaplain should not be looking for converts or followers, and should be vigilant to even the subtlest signs that such motives are creeping in. This is especially critical for chaplains from traditions with an outreach focus.

CHAPLAIN IN INTERFAITH

As chaplaincy becomes an increasingly multi-faith field, opportunities for co-operation on issues of pastoral care also increases. There are many possibilities for collaboration in interfaith worship, client case-work, humanitarian projects, and sharing resources.

One role that Hindu chaplains might assume in an interfaith context is as a mediator of Hinduism. Hindus in the diaspora generally enjoy cordial and mutually supportive relationships with people of other faiths. Nonetheless, relationships between religious institutions and communities can be complex and sometimes even problematic. A Hindu chaplain may need to help members of his or her community to find their place in an interfaith world.

Many see religion as a cause of conflict, some conflicts we observe today appear to be linked to religious differences. A study of history suggests, however, that religion is rarely the primary cause of conflict and is invoked to provide legitimacy for acts of aggression with economic and political causes. Nonetheless, such conflicts may be a source of division between religious communities and the chaplain may have to confront these divisions.

Another potential source of conflict is tensions around issues of exclusivity and conversion. This is particularly the case where a religious tradition claims exclusive access to revealed truth and on this basis finds justification for seeking to convert people of other faiths. Often, when mission-driven faiths such as Christianity and Islam have encountered Hindus they have regarded it as a form of gross error. In recent years, however many have moved beyond their exclusivist positions and often work with other faiths without any imperative toward conversion. Interfaith groups offer people of faith the opportunity to work together in a spirit of cooperation and mutual appreciation and as such provide many opportunities for chaplains. The Hindu chaplain can be an exemplar of working with other people of faith, and can encourage his or her community members to do likewise.

Sometimes, the Hindu chaplain may still be called upon to help Hindus respond to efforts at proselytisation. In some cases, he or she can help Hindus to appreciate the sincere intention of those attempting to preach to them, while helping them to respond respectfully. The chaplain can also help clarify doubts or answer criticisms of Hinduism made by others.

Misunderstandings may exist around differences between faiths. For instance, some may take exception to murti puja (the worship of sacred images) and other rituals that are so important to many Hindus. In addition, followers of staunchly monotheistic traditions may exclude or criticise Hindus as being polytheists – which, as we have already noted, is an over-simplification and a misunderstanding of the different ways that Hindu traditions express the complexity of divinity. These are opportunities for Hindu chaplains to educate others about Hindu belief and practice. He or she can confront stereotypes and help to correct inaccurate information. The chaplain can also help members of the Hindu community become more comfortable with representing themselves with clarity and confidence. The goal is not to gloss over real differences between the faiths, but rather to engage in constructive and respectful dialogue about them; the chaplain can model and encourage such dialogue.

Hindus may on occasion experience tension with members of other faiths around historical conflicts. Here, again, the chaplain can help Hindus to navigate such tension. For instance, although Hindus today generally enjoy good relations with Christians, the legacy of the colonial period remains. Similarly, the history of India and partition, ongoing conflicts in Kashmir, communal violence, and acts of terrorism, have sometimes soured relations between Hindus and sections of the Islamic community. While the Hindu chaplain need not be a historian or an apologist, he or she should be aware of, and sensitive to, the history underlying contemporary tensions.

There is no quick fix to issues of religious tension, and it is unfair and unrealistic to expect a chaplain to 'solve the problem' on behalf of the community. Rather, the chaplain can model healthy ways of acknowledging and engaging with the tension. In doing so, the Hindu chaplain can draw from Hinduism's tendency toward pluralism, tolerance, and interreligious cooperation. We have already touched upon the diversity that exists within Hindu belief and practice; at this point we might simply note again that Hindus may hold to various patterns of belief. This mood of acceptance is not simply a matter of convenience based on the presence of diversity; it is also a matter of doctrine. There are, for instance, Advaitins, Vaishnavas, Shaivites, Shaktas, and many others who somehow manage to combine the beliefs and practices of all these traditions. Remarkably, the larger umbrella tradition that has come to be known as Hinduism has managed to maintain a great deal of diversity within itself, and with few but notable exceptions, in a harmonious spirit. For instance, it is quite possible to be a Hindu without believing in God, as the Samkhya and Mimamsa systems demonstrate; on the other hand, for other Hindus, such as Vaishnavas or Vira Shaivas, the personal deity remains at the heart of religious and spiritual life. Moreover, Hinduism includes a range of established sects, each of which will have its own canon, institutional forms, and particular beliefs and practices. We might even be tempted to think of these as distinct religions. Yet still these diverse groups see themselves as Hindu, and are often happy sharing a common identity with others whose beliefs may be very different from their own.

That is not to say that religious disputation is unknown in the Hindu tradition, for we can find numerous examples of polemical writing and traditions of vigorous debate between rival sects or schools of philosophy. Such disputation is, however, largely confined to the intellectual sphere; in practice, there are few substantial divisions between adherents of sects or traditions within Hinduism. This tolerance of diversity naturally lends itself to the way that Hindus might approach the followers of faiths other than Hinduism. The Hindu chaplain might remind the members of his or her community that Hindus intrinsically demonstrate a remarkable capacity to accept other religions.

This inclusive perspective is not only derived from the internal diversity of Hinduism, but also forms a significant part of Hindu teachings. A Hindu chaplain can refer to these, upholding the validity of different stages of spiritual development and different expressions of religion. For example, in a significant passage from the Bhagavad-gita, Krishna affirms a multiplicity of paths:

ye yatha mam prapadyante
tams tathaiva bhajamy aham
mama vartmanuvartante
manushyah partha sarvashah

> In the way that they become dependent upon me, so I devote myself to them. In all circumstances, Partha, people follow the path I set for them. (Bhagavad-gita 4.11)

This verse indicates that different expressions of religion are not mutually contradictory, but rather different ways of surrendering to God. The Gita passage does not suggest that all paths are the same or pretend that differences do not exist, but it does acknowledge and affirm a plurality of paths.

In another passage, Krishna also affirms the sanctity of a person's choice:

iti te jñanam akhyatam
guhyad guhyattamam maya
vimrishyaitad asheshena
yathecchasi tatha kuru

> I have now revealed to you this wisdom, which is the deepest mystery. After fully considering what you have heard, you should then act as you see fit. (Bhagavad-gita 18.63)

This verse comes at the very conclusion of the Bhagavad-gita. The significant point here is that although Krishna, the supreme deity, has given instruction to Arjuna, he does not demand that his word be obeyed to the very letter. Arjuna is asked to reflect deeply on what he has heard and then use his intelligence to determine his path. On reading the Gita, different people will reach different conclusions as to how its ideas can be implemented. Some will make different choices to ourselves, but these decisions are to be respected and not condemned as falsehoods. We can easily see the benefits of carrying this sense of respecting individual choice into the realm of interreligious understanding.

This does not, however, mean that Hinduism and Hindus will accept any form or expression of religion as valid. There is a broad acceptance of religious diversity but there are also limits that are dictated by the core values of dharma we discussed earlier. Again in the Bhagavad-gita, we find this statement:

adharmam dharmam iti ya
manyante tamasavritah
sarvarthan viparitams cha
buddhih sa partha tamasi

> But where the intellect is covered by darkness (tamas), it considers adharma to be dharma, and has wrong conceptions on all subjects. This is the intellect dominated by tamas. (Bhagavad-gita 18.32)

Here Krishna refers to persons absorbed in darkness and ignorance, under the sway of the quality known as tamas. Such persons represent adharma, or wickedness, as dharma. Where dharma is clearly breached and destructive acts performed in the name of religion, then limits must be imposed. This is as applicable to Hindus as it is to followers of other faiths. In broad terms, most followers of the major religions share the values espoused by the teachings on dharma, and hence there is much common ground for Hindus and adherents of other faiths to build on. Hinduism is particularly inclined towards this mood of cooperation.

At its best then, Hinduism can offer an antidote to the

attitudes that challenge cooperation between religions. Jews, Christians, Muslims, and Zoroastrians all found refuge in India under the aegis of Hindu rulers, and were allowed to practise their faith without any attempt at conversion. This is Hinduism at its best. There have also been many incidents where Hindus have participated in or incited religiously-motivated violence. Ideally, however, the precepts of the tradition should naturally move Hindus towards tolerance, acceptance, and peaceful co-existence.

CHAPLAIN AS ADVISOR

In addition to providing spiritual care and guidance in the ways we have already discussed, the Hindu chaplain might also play an advisory role to Hindu professionals in other fields. For our purposes, we can look at two such fields – health care and business.

Before we turn to specific ways that the chaplain might be helpful in advising Hindus in these fields, we might do well to turn again to the Bhagavad-gita's teachings on karma-yoga. Starting from the position Arjuna finds himself in on the battlefield, the Gita proceeds to explain how a life of seemingly worldly action can be compatible with the spiritual path that aims at liberation from rebirth. For the Bhagavad-gita, it is important that even those with a strong inclination towards spiritual pursuits continue to be active in the world so that society can flourish and prosper. Therefore, the karma-yoga it recommends involves performing one's duties while remaining detached from the material result or the duality of success and failure. The Gita upholds the Hindu virtues of non-attachment and renunciation – but does so with regard to attitude rather than activity or occupation. To paraphrase these teachings in most basic terms, the Gita reassures us that one can be 'in this world but not of it' and that work performed in this consciousness connects us with our deepest spiritual essence.

While the notion of karma-yoga may seem straightforward and simple in theory, it can be challenging to apply these teachings in high-intensity, demanding professions. Thus, Hindu chaplains may provide an important service as advisors to those in such professions. Healthcare professionals such as physicians, nurses, and therapists must often confront stark experiences of illness and loss. A chaplain can draw on the idea of karma-yoga to help such professionals explore how their work can be a part of, and even an expression of, their personal spirituality. In fact, work that involves care and help for others in need can readily be applied to the doctrine of karma-yoga, for such work will often be motivated by the ideal of serving others rather the desire for personal gain.

For those who work as nurses or doctors, or in any field where care for others is a principal function, we can note again the close relationship between compassion and Sanatana Dharma. One might even say that these professions become a part of religious life because the attitude and mentality required are the very essence of dharma. The Hindu chaplain can help persons working in these fields to see their work as part of their spiritual practice, and thus encourage these professionals to approach both in an integrated way. At the same time, as we have already seen in the context of the military, those tasked with serving others often neglect their own needs in the process. Chaplains can be helpful in reminding caregivers to make self-care a priority, and in providing resources from the tradition to aid in this self-care. For instance, in the Bhagavad-gita, Krishna advises one on the spiritual path to adopt moderation in sleep, diet, and even recreation (6.17). The chaplain might use passages such as this to explore work–life balance and healthy sleep habits, diet, exercise, spiritual practice, personal relationships, and so on.

But what of those in business and industry? Might a chaplain be of benefit here? Indeed, a number of companies have recognised the important role of pastoral care and advice and have added chaplains to their staffs to provide this service.

Hindu chaplains serving in such contexts can offer much the same guidance we have discussed in our exploration of the healthcare field. Work–life balance and self-care are also important issues within the business world. And, at its best, the corporate sphere can also be a field in which to practise karma-yoga. According to Hindu teachings, dharmic trade calls for business leaders to go beyond the pursuit of raw profit and to see their role as servants of the community who provide employment for others and prosperity for society as a whole.

How can chaplains help translate this ideal into practice? One way is to help explore the relationship between Hindu teachings and business ethics. As managers and employers, as well as the financial backbone for society, business leaders can have a profound influence over the lives of others – and thus it is critical that they operate from a set of values as a firm basis. We have seen recently in the banking industry how a lack of respect for fundamental values can have disastrous consequences. Let us then remind ourselves of the core values that comprise Sanatana Dharma and briefly consider how they apply to business. These verses are from the Mahabharata:

adrohah sarva-bhuteshu
karmana manasa gira
anugrahas cha danam cha
satam dharmah sanatanah

> Never displaying malice towards any living being through actions, thoughts or words, acts of kindness, and giving charity; this is the Sanatana Dharma adhered to by righteous persons. (Mahabharata 3.281.34)

ahimsa satyam akrodho
danam etac chatushtaya
ajata-shatro sevasva
dharma esha sanatanah

> Not harming, truthfulness, remaining free from anger, and charity, are the four practices you must adhere to, Ajatashatru. This is the Sanatana Dharma. (Mahabharata 13.147.22)

It is clear from these passages, and there are several others like them in other Hindu sacred texts, that the defining values of Sanatana Dharma can greatly inform decision-making in business. For instance, employers and business leaders may at times have to sanction those who work for them, but Sanatana Dharma dictates that this should not be done harshly, and only as a matter of necessity, reluctantly, and without malice or anger. A mood of non-attachment, kindness, and non-harming should ideally permeate all our work environments, however trying the situation may be. A particularly relevant value for business is the quality of *satyam*, generally translated as truthfulness or honesty, but understood more broadly as integrity. In our dealings, business and personal, there will at times be a temptation to act deceptively or to take advantage of others in order to secure our own advantage, but the teachings on dharma insist that our actions evince *satyam.* For the Hindu, 'honesty is the best policy' is not merely a truism or a good business strategy – it is integral to living a life consistent with dharma.

Echoing the verses we have cited from the Mahabharata are numerous references, parables, and narratives. For example, the Hindu king Harishchandra is often praised as the epitome of *satyam* and an exemplar of dharmic leadership; even when tested by the gods and subjected to extreme circumstances, he upheld *satyam* to such an extent that his name has become synonymous with truthfulness. Similarly, the life of Sri Rama is often cited as a further illustration of the relationship between dharma and honesty. While these narratives may not speak directly to modern business, their teachings on dharma are still relevant to the formulation of Hindu business ethics.

Another relevant characteristic of Sanatana Dharma is the obligation to give in charity. This instruction is especially meant for householders living and working in the secular world – that is to say, most of us. The idea is that giving in charity helps to balance the accumulation of wealth and pursuit of profit with a responsibility to care for others. In the Bhagavad-gita, Krishna declares giving in charity to be a divine quality that must be performed:

yajna-dana-tapah-karma
na tyajyam karyam eva tat
yajno danam tapas chaiva
pavanani manishinam

etany api tu karmani
sangam tyaktva phalani cha
kartavyaniti me partha
nischitam matam uttamam

> Acts of ritual sacrifice, charity, and austerity must not be given up. Rather, they must be performed, for it is sacrifice, charity, and austerity that purify men of wisdom. Renouncing attachment and the rewards of action, one must perform this type of action. This is my ultimate conclusion, Partha. (Bhagavad-gita 18.5–6)

Significantly, even while he calls us to perform acts of charity, Krishna also reminds us that it is not simply the *act* of giving that is important – it is the consciousness in which the charity is given and the motives behind it that matter. He expands on this idea in a passage that is especially relevant to those in the professional sphere:

datavyam iti yad danam
diyate 'nupakarine
dese kale cha patre cha
tad danam sattvikam smritam

yat tu pratyupakarartham
phalam uddisya va punah
diyate cha pariklishtam
tad danam rajasam smritam

adesa-kale yad danam
apatrebhyas cha diyate
asat-kritam avajnatam
tat tamasam udahritam

> Charity which is given with the thought, 'This should be given' and is presented to a suitable recipient from whom nothing is expected in return, at the right time and place, is of the nature of *sattva*.
>
> But that charity which is given with the expectation of getting something in return, for some subsequent result, or with reluctance, is of the nature of *rajas*.
>
> And that charity which is given at the wrong place and wrong time to an unsuitable recipient, which is given improperly or with contempt, is of the nature of *tamas*. (Bhagavad-gita 17.20–22)

How might a professional seeking to follow Krishna's teachings do so? Here, a chaplain may be an advisor and conversation partner. And while we generally think of giving in charity in individual terms, we can expand this idea of 'appropriate charity' to apply to responsible, beneficial, and sustainable business practices generally. Here too, a chaplain can be a resource in helping translate Hindu ideals into practice.

The modern world is dominated by business interests that influence all our lives. Many people feel resentment against the business community and criticise the manner in which some businesses seek to expand their profits. The Hindu tradition and its ancient teachings may appear, at first glance, to be distanced from such tensions but, as we have seen from this brief discussion, it can make vital contributions to our understanding of how business should be conducted in a manner that is both ethical and beneficial to all. Sanatana Dharma teachings can provide a powerful alternative to the status quo. As one contemporary Hindu swami phrased it, while recently addressing young leaders in the corporate world: 'Dharma in business means earning with integrity, and spending with wisdom and compassion.'

We might refer again to the Hindu understanding that there are four principal goals of life – *kama, artha, dharma,* and *moksha.* Being a professional thus means to some extent, juggling these pursuits. Hindu teaching does not condemn the pursuit of wealth, *artha*, or the enjoyment that comes with it, *kama*; rather, the teaching reminds us that these two must be governed by *dharma* and, ultimately, seen in the larger perspective of *moksha*. Avaricious tendencies must be tempered by a respect for the precepts of dharma. It is here that striking a balance is most significant, and the Hindu chaplain can help others to do that.

CHAPLAIN AS COMMUNITY BUILDER

The final role we will examine in this session – but a vital one in the diaspora – is that of community builder. As a community builder, the chaplain may be called on to play a host of roles – translator, facilitator, mediator, unifier, coordinator, and mentor.

To meaningfully examine the emerging importance of the Hindu chaplain as a community builder, we must first look at the context of that community in diaspora. Hinduism today remains overwhelmingly a 'religion of India' with strong associations with that region. Over the past fifty years or so, however, we have seen the emergence of significant Hindu communities in the Western world, in countries such as the USA, Britain, Canada, Australia, and those of the EU. This development is the result of mass migration but it is not an exclusively modern phenomenon; earlier diaspora communities existed, and still exist, in various parts of the old British Empire, in South Africa, Kenya, Uganda, Fiji, Trinidad, and Mauritius. These communities are still strong and thriving, and have a rather different experience of diaspora. In some cases there has been dual migration whereby families moved initially within the British Empire and then two or three generations later moved again to Europe, Australasia, or North America. This occurred most notably amongst communities settled in East Africa where their situation became less favourable following independence from Britain in the 1960s.

If we focus on the communities that have developed and taken root in Britain and other European countries, we can observe that the primary migrations occurred in the 1960s and 1970s. This is significant for our discussion of chaplaincy, because it means that many diaspora communities are now three or four generations old, although there are still some immigrants who have arrived from India more recently. There are today over one million Hindus in the USA and perhaps 200,000 in Canada, whilst in Europe the largest community is in Britain, followed by the Netherlands, Italy, and France.

Each of these groups has its own identity. In Britain, many of the families migrated from East Africa but retain a strong Gujarati or Punjabi identity. It is estimated that around 70% of British Hindus are of Gujarati background and 20% Punjabi, with the remaining 10% made up of smaller communities from other parts of India. In the Netherlands, most Hindus migrated from Suriname and are of a North Indian background, notably from Uttar Pradesh and Bihar. These histories are important in understanding diaspora communities, since regional distinctions often inform a community's expression of Hinduism, sometimes even more than theological or sectarian ones. For example, devotion to Krishna and to Rama is prominent amongst Gujarati and Punjabi Hindus; the Swaminarayan sect has a significant following amongst those of a Gujarati background; and Arya Samaj has a significant following amongst Punjabis. As we touched on in the introductory session, the Hindu identity is multi-layered and complex. Language, culture, religion are all part of a fluid whole. The Hindu chaplain must engage with it all. Chaplains would thus be well advised to research these regional distinctions in the country in which they are working in order to get a deeper understanding of the expressions of Hinduism they are most likely to come in contact with.

One of the main features of the development of these communities is the change in first language from an Indian language such as Hindi or Gujarati to English or the local European language. What we can observe is that for the elders of the family, the native language is still widely used; the second generation, however, are generally equally fluent in their mother tongue and the host country's language, and can use them interchangeably. For the third and later generations, the host country's language is generally the first language, and some find it quite difficult to communicate freely in the Indian native language used by previous generations. Efforts may be made to teach children the language of the older generations but even where successful it is likely to remain as a second tongue, for occasional use only.

This discussion of language use in the diaspora is important for us, not just because it relates to effective communication, but also because of the close relationship between language and culture, and hence language and religion. Those who have grown up in a diaspora environment, and who think and speak in a European language, have undergone significant acculturation. Thus, the Hinduism practised by older generations may no longer appear comprehensible, relevant, or even appropriate. Moreover, the values and lifestyle choices adopted by younger Hindus, influenced by Western culture, may be radically different from those of their parents and grandparents, and this can lead to tensions and disagreements within families. Young people who have grown up and been educated in the Western world may not accept the instruction of parents, and will often ask for explanations of religious ethics and practice. One Hindu woman contrasted her experience growing up in India with that of her British-born children: 'When I was young, we asked our parents "what?" questions, but our children ask us "why?" questions and very often we don't know the answers.'

What this suggests is that, unless they are given a way of making sense of it, younger generations may begin to see their religion and culture as outdated and irrelevant.

How can the Hindu chaplain serve as a community builder in this context? He or she may act as a translator, sometimes literally, but more often metaphorically. In this respect, the role of the chaplain might be to explain the relevance of Hindu ideas and values to the modern world. He or she may need to translate between languages, but also between cultural and generational paradigms. The task chaplains must face is that of giving advice and guidance, particularly to the younger generations, in a non-dogmatic way that will make sense to the mind shaped by Western culture. It is not enough merely to recite traditional teachings; chaplains must be able to make their words relevant by applying the tradition and its values to the living issues of the modern world.

Hindu chaplains are also community builders in terms of engaging with questions of adaptation and assimilation. Regardless of ethnic or religious backgrounds, all diaspora communities must grapple with decisions as to how far integration and adaptation should prevail over preserving tradition and maintaining orthodoxy. Muslim, Sikh, and Hindu communities living in the diaspora seek prosperity and harmony in their new environment, and this is often most easily achieved by abandoning traditional cultures and accepting those of the Western world. And yet, these communities also struggle with the fear of losing their identities and thus realise the importance of preserving and passing down tradition. Hence there is a balance to be negotiated and difficult decisions to be made. Hindu chaplains can be an integral part of this process, helping communities to discern which traditions and values are fundamental or essential to religious commitment, and which are secondary or open to greater interpretation and change. Generally, Hindu communities in the Western world have been open to such change. We can observe, for example, how some traditional rules relating to caste or marriage have in many cases been modified, re-interpreted, or even set aside, as they no longer appear relevant or meaningful to the community. In this, the Hindu chaplain is fortunate to be working with adherents of a religious tradition that is not overly rooted in scriptural dogma and which has the ability to transform and develop in line with the social environments in which it takes root.

Chaplains might also play the role of mediators, especially between generations of Hindus. Many young Hindus are no longer interested in caste identity and some are actively opposed to such ideas. Similarly, marriage arrangements are now only rarely left to the parents to decide. Young diaspora Hindus often question restrictions that their parents and grandparents took for granted. In some cases, they engage in activities that previous generations considered taboo, such as premarital sex or the consumption of alcohol.

Most Hindu parents accept that their children will structure their lives differently from their own, and this will increasingly become the case. At the same time, tensions may arise between generations that will require thoughtful mediating. Many young Hindus in diaspora have had to develop expertise in negotiating the cultural disparity between their non-Hindu peers and the elders of their family. Hindu chaplains – particularly younger chaplains from similar backgrounds – will be invaluable allies in this process of negotiation and navigation.

Another reality of the diaspora is that the *mandir*, or temple, has grown beyond being solely a place for the ritual worship that is such a prominent feature of Hinduism. Rather it has come to function as a community centre providing a range of services for Hindus of all ages. For instance, many temples host Hindu youth-group meetings. The services offered by these temples extend to the secular as well. In some temples, additional tutoring is provided to help young Hindus with their school examinations. At the large Swaminarayan temple in Neasden, London, there is a gymnasium where young people can play football and other sports. These and other activities can help provide a real sense of community, and whenever possible chaplains should try to become involved with them in various different ways. To achieve this, they might try to build close ties and good relations with the leaders of the different temples and community centres, and work with them in establishing suitable community activities.

As a community builder, the chaplain may also be called on to serve as a facilitator and coordinator of programmes. There is often a tendency among younger Hindus to regard Hindu beliefs, values, and traditions as irrelevant. Hindu chaplains can address this in a number of ways. For instance, chaplains can organise and promote discussions to explore how Hindu values are important for life in the modern world. They can encourage young people to make presentations, and invite guest speakers to share perspectives on the faith. While possessing a wide-ranging body of background knowledge will certainly be helpful, the role of the chaplain here is primarily that of the facilitator. The most important consideration is to allow a diversity of voices to be heard, and to create an environment that will encourage young Hindus to participate.

Sometimes, tensions arise between different regional, institutional, or sectarian groups resulting in divisions within the Hindu community as a whole. In his or her capacity as a community builder, a Hindu chaplain can act as a link between these groups, encouraging joint activities and cooperative ventures. The chaplain can advocate working together on commonly held concerns and, if possible, joint performance of rituals. In this context, it is important that the chaplain not be regarded as representing one particular community or temple, and he or she must ensure equal attention is paid to as many groups as possible. This will be especially challenging when the chaplain identifies with a particular tradition or organisation in his or her own spiritual practice. Here, self-awareness, transparency, honesty, and sensitivity are key.

We have already seen that charity and philanthropy are important aspects of Hindu culture and so another significant way chaplains may serve as community builders is in relation to philanthropic activities.

The chaplain can play a vital role in organising such initiatives and in explaining how they form an integral part of the dharma taught by the ancient Hindu texts. Many Hindu groups today engage in fundraising for educational and welfare projects – in India in particular – and chaplains can help connect these projects with community members. This can be especially powerful for young Hindus, who may otherwise find it difficult to relate to the faith. As we will discuss later, Hinduism has a rich tradition of ritual worship, but many young Hindus find the ritual aspects to be less compelling or relevant to them and the world around them. By helping community members engage with charitable work, a Hindu chaplain can show that Sanatana Dharma is more than simply ritual or philosophy, and entails action for the benefit of others and in the mood of care and compassion.

For instance, in the wake of the earthquakes that recently devastated Nepal, a group of young Hindu-Americans (some with direct ties to Nepal) reached out to their chaplain. While some wanted to explore the pastoral dimensions to the tragedy or asked for guidance in coping with it, most were more interested in how they could be helpful to relief efforts on the ground. They looked to the chaplain to help them coordinate these efforts, but also to affirm that their actions were part of their faith as Hindus.

CONCLUSION

This exploration of the roles played by Hindu chaplains reveals a larger reality about contemporary Hinduism in the diaspora. In essence, what we are seeing emerge is a new form of Hinduism – based undoubtedly on traditional teachings and values, but particularly relevant to the concerns of the modern world.

Even as certain traditional aspects of the Hindu religion might seem less important today, in their place other strands of the tradition come to the fore. Whereas previous generations might have placed greater importance on ritual and caste duties, contemporary Hindu communities might instead emphasise inner spirituality, work–life balance, and welfare activities on behalf of all other beings who share the world with us. This is a fluid and dynamic process, and will require thoughtful negotiation and reflection. In building and strengthening community ties, the Hindu chaplain can play a vital role in the process.

3. HINDUISM AND RITUAL

In previous sessions, we looked in broad terms at the roles that Hindu chaplains play, and discussed how they might draw from Hindu teachings to serve in these roles. We also explored the tensions that chaplains must negotiate, and help other Hindus to negotiate, as the teachings and practices of tradition intersect with modernity.

We now look more closely at the significance of ritual in Hinduism. To explore this important and vast subject, we begin with an admittedly cursory historical overview to offer us context. We then discuss Hindu perspectives on the significance, benefit, and limitations of ritual. We will balance this with an anthropological look at ritual in traditional Indian and diaspora contexts. Finally, we consider why exploration of, and engagement with, ritual is important for the Hindu chaplain.

THE HISTORICAL PERSPECTIVE

The Vedic ritual

From the earliest times, ritual has been an essential feature of the religious traditions now known collectively as Hinduism. The earliest texts we have reveal that the Vedas are primarily ritualistic works, outlining the manner in which the *yajña*, or fire sacrifice, is to be performed; the role of different classes of priests; the gods to be worshipped; and the hymns to be chanted alongside each part of the ritual.

The aim behind this ritual seems to have been primarily pragmatic, being focused on good fortune and prosperity. Some prayers do seek to elevate the performer in the afterlife, but for the most part the ritual is concerned with fertility, the coming of the rains, and gaining victory over enemies. The complexity of the Vedic ritual is such that it requires a class of specialist priests, brahmins, who have studied the Vedas and committed large sections to memory. The ritual must be perfectly enacted as any mistake or shortcoming will reduce its efficacy.

The Upanishads and tensions over ritual practice

We could spend more time considering the details of the Vedic ritual, but at this point it is sufficient for us to note the salience of ritual in Vedic Hinduism, a factor that continues to the present day, though in rather changed forms. We should also be aware that within the Vedas, the Upanishad portion offers an alternative to the ritualism found elsewhere. To some extent, this portion stands in tension with the emphasis on ritual. On numerous occasions, the Upanishads reveal that there is an esoteric meaning behind the ritual, and assert that the true aim of religious practice should be transcendence of the world through higher knowledge, rather than control of natural forces through ritual means. The first chapter of the Kena Upanishad, for instance, is a striking example of this shift in emphasis. This is not to say that the Upanishads are opposed to ritual acts, but rather that they seek something beyond ritual. For these texts, beyond ritual there is the search for a higher reality, an explanation for our existence, and the means by which the world can ultimately be transcended. This tendency away from ritual and toward transcendence is something we can also recognise in the Buddhist traditions.

At this point, we should take special note of the Bhagavad-gita, which was compiled some centuries after the major Upanishads. We have considered the importance of the Gita throughout the previous sessions, and here too its teachings shed some light. The Gita is by no means opposed to the performance of the Vedic ritual – just the opposite, as verses 3.11–15 make clear. At the same time, it does offer a sharp rebuff to those – especially those of the priestly class – who might assert that ritual alone would suffice. It is helpful to look at a section in the second chapter of the Gita:

yam imam pushpitam vacham
pravadanty avipaschitah
veda-vada-ratah partha
nanyad astiti vadinah

kamatmanah svarga-para
janma-karma-phala-pradam
kriya-visesha-bahulam
bhogaisvarya-gatim prati

bhogaisvarya-prasaktanam
tayapahrita-cetasam
vyavasayatmika buddhih
samadhau na vidhiyate

traigunya-vishaya veda
nistraigunyo bhavarjuna
nirdvandvo nitya-sattva-stho
niryoga-kshema atmavan

yavan artha udapane
sarvatah samplutodake
tavan sarveshu vedeshu
brahmanasya vijanatah

> Persons lacking in insight, who are attached to the religion of the Vedas, speak in flowery language. 'There is nothing more than this,' they say.

Filled with desires, and seeking the heavenly worlds, they advocate many different types of ritual, which lead to a higher birth as the result of such actions. Pleasure and power are the goals they seek.

The resolute form of intelligence existing in the state of samadhi can never arise for such persons, who remain attached to pleasure and power and whose minds are carried away by such desires.

The Vedas are permeated by the three *gunas*, but you must become free of the three *gunas*, Arjuna. One who is self-possessed transcends all duality, always adheres to the quality of *sattva*, and has no interest in gain or protection of property.

All the purposes served by a small reservoir of water can be fulfilled by a lake. In the same way, the purposes served by all the Vedas are fulfilled for a brahmin who is enlightened by knowledge. (Bhagavad-gita, 2.42–6)

This short passage is clear in its critique of an overemphasis on ritual, but there are a few points in particular that we should notice. Firstly, the passage argues that ritual alone is not enough. The persons being critiqued here, the *veda-vada-ratas*, are those who claim that ritual alone is sufficient for a religious life. In historical terms, we might see this passage as reflecting the debates between the ritualists who adhered to the *mimamsaka* system and the proponents of Vedanta who insist on the precedence of realised knowledge. The Bhagavad-gita holds to the view that while ritual is important and must not be whimsically rejected or denigrated, ritual alone is not enough, for knowledge and realisation are the higher goals. A second point this passage makes is that the benefits provided by ritual follow concomitantly from the pursuit of metaphysics and meditation. At the end of the passage, in verse 46, Krishna insists that one who possesses genuine spiritual realisation has no need to perform the ritual separately, for all his spiritual goals are already fulfilled. In other words, a person who pursues the goal of spiritual knowledge need only aspire toward realisation, without worrying about additionally endeavouring for perfection in performing ritual.

A final point to note from this section of the Gita is that Krishna classifies the Vedas and the Vedic ritual as being a feature of the three *gunas*, the three pervasive qualities on which the material domain is based, which Arjuna is advised to transcend. Hence, the Gita is asserting that the Vedic ritual is not a purely spiritual practice, but something that is a part of this world. According to the Upanishads, a different means is required for the purpose of transcendence, and the Bhagavad-gita shares this view.

Temple ritual

So far our discussion has focused on the Vedic ritual. However, in contemporary Hindu practice most of the rituals enacted are temple-based and derived from non-Vedic sources. Temples and temple ritual postdates the Vedic period by several centuries, and it is likely that the rituals of image worship did not become prominent until as late as the 5th or 6th centuries AD. At about this time, Indian religion was transformed by the rapid growth of monotheistic traditions, most notably those dedicated to Vishnu and Shiva, in which intense devotion to a single deity became the most prominent feature. These traditions developed their own systems of ritual, and compiled texts governing those rituals known collectively as tantra.

Tantra is a term that has been misused in recent years. Tantra refers to a series of ritual practices by means of which it is believed that a material object can be transformed into something spiritual. This transformation can apply to the image of the deity worshipped in the temple, the *murti*, or to the human body by means of yoga. The image worshipped in the temple is regarded by some Hindus as purely symbolic, an object on which the worshippers can fix their minds, but the traditional belief is that the image is transformed by ritual into a living embodiment of the deity. From that moment, anything offered to the sacred image becomes itself a sacred object that can bestow material and spiritual benefits. Other than a few exceptional communities and movements which intentionally draw from the Vedic conception of ritual, most contemporary Hindus engage with ritual, to some extent, in this way.

Thus we can observe that the type of rituals performed has changed markedly. Hindu ritual today centres on the worship of sacred images within the temple. Almost every town and village in India has a temple supervised by brahmin priests, alongside other shrines of a less formal nature. Hindus regularly make pilgrimages to the largest and most famous temples, many of which are in South India. Meanwhile, diaspora communities have established temples in Western cities. In these temples, one will generally find the same rituals of image worship conducted by brahmin priests, who are usually brought from India with knowledge of ritual practices. In the West, however, the priests are generally not the owners or proprietors of the temples, but are effectively employees of the management committees, which have overall charge of the premises, its functions, and its finances.

HINDU PERSPECTIVES ON THE SIGNIFICANCE OF RITUAL

It is, of course, misleading to speak of a singular Hindu perspective on anything – least of all a subject as diverse and layered as ritual. Rather, we are likely to find a number of different ways Hindus look at and engage with ritual.

Many Hindus, for instance, believe in the efficacy of ritual in producing the results they seek in terms of well-being, prosperity, and relief from suffering. Some Hindus also enact rituals on behalf of departed parents and loved ones, in order to not only bring them good fortune in their next life, but also as a way of remembering the lives of the departed and the happy times shared with them. Other Hindus, however, are more sceptical about the performance of ritual, and doubt its potency. This scepticism is frequently combined with the view that the priests are motivated primarily by financial gain, which in turn leads to a lack of respect for their profession and practice. The influence of modern scientific knowledge has also led to some scepticism about the power of ritual. A further factor to consider is that many Hindus believe that the highest spiritual goals are achieved through knowledge, realisation, and ultimate enlightenment – not through rituals. Here too, there may be differences of opinion; while some may condemn ritual, most Hindus agree that since the majority of people have not yet reached a stage where enlightenment is possible, ritual may be helpful in bringing about the purification that is a required prerequisite for enlightenment.

As we saw earlier, most Hindus are inclined towards the devotional forms of the religion that have been such a powerful force in shaping the culture and lifestyle of the Indian subcontinent. This devotion is often expressed through the rituals of temple worship. Vaishnavas, Shaivites, and Shaktas (worshippers of Vishnu, Shiva, and the Goddess respectively) have all established temples in which images of the deity are worshipped. For many Hindus, the ritual and the image provide a focus for their devotional sentiments.

With this brief survey as a background, let us examine how Hindus understand the purposes of ritual, how they relate to ritual priests, and how they view the role of ritual in light of modernity.

Purposes served by ritual

Our earlier discussion about the tensions between ritual and transcendence focused on Vedic ritual. Vedic ritual is still practised today, though not on the same scale as in ancient times, and it is typically combined with rituals derived from later sources. The attitudes toward ritual that are evident in the Upanishads and the Bhagavad-gita, and the arguments about the limitations of ritual we saw in the Bhagavad-gita, do, however, still apply. Ritual remains a prominent feature of contemporary Hinduism, but there are many Hindus who feel that an excessive emphasis on ritual can detract from the spirituality that is the true essence of their religion. That spirituality can take the form of the quest for realised knowledge or of intense devotion to God, both focused on something beyond this world, and Hindus perform ritual worship as part of this pursuit. At the same time, Hindus often balance this 'other-worldly' aspiration with performing ritual for pragmatic purposes relating to prosperity and well-being in this world. This is not usually condemned for being materialistic, but Hindus generally accept that the purely spiritual or unmotivated forms of religion, including ritual acts, are of a higher order. This is again confirmed in the Bhagavad-gita:

chatur-vidha bhajante mam
janah sukritino 'rjuna
arto jijñasur artharthi
jñani cha bharatarshabha

tesham jñani nitya-yukta
eka-bhaktir visishyate
priyo hi jñanino 'tyartham
aham sa cha mama priyah

> Four types of righteous person worship me, Arjuna: one who is in distress, one who wishes to understand, one who seeks prosperity, and the *jñanin* who possesses knowledge, O best of the Bharatas.
>
> The one possessing knowledge (*jñanin*), who is always properly engaged and has single-pointed devotion, is the best of these. I am very dear to such a *jñanin* and he is dear to me. (Bhagavad-gita 7.16–17)

There are a number of points here we might note, but the main idea we want to focus on is that the Gita recognises that different motivations may impel one to perform ritual worship. Worship can be undertaken by those who need help or desire prosperity; it can also be a recognition of God's sovereignty or purely an expression of love of God. Although the text clearly favours this latter motivation as spiritually superior, the more pragmatic forms of worship are not condemned or dismissed. Indeed all the worshippers are designated as *sukritins*, righteous persons. Where rituals of worship are performed today, the same principle applies. They may be undertaken with some specific aim, or they may purely be expressions of the worshippers' love and dedication to the deity. The ritual fulfils both functions. The prayers of the South Indian Vaishnava poets, the Alvars, refer repeatedly to the temples they visit, as do the works of the Shaivite Nayanmars, with their outpourings of devotional sentiment. At the same time, many acts of ritual are performed within those same temples with worldly goals in mind. Both functions are essential features of the Hindu ritual life, and the chaplain must be aware of and respect this dual purpose.

As we touched on in our brief historical overview, Hindu ritual today takes many different forms. These forms include the Vedic sacrifice, the *yajña,* most commonly performed today for special occasions such as marriage ceremonies, other rites of passage, purification, or the dedication of a new home. For many Hindus, this is the extent of their engagement with Vedic ritual; they are more likely to encounter Hindu ritual in a temple. Of course there are some important exceptions to this generalisation, and a few particular communities or members of Vedic revivalist groups – the Arya Samaj and the Gayatri Parivar are two notable examples – do perform Vedic sacrifice more frequently and as a primary practice. Although most of these rituals are performed by experienced brahmin priests, it would be useful for the chaplain to gain an understanding of their meaning so he or she can provide an explanation of the rites.

The role of brahmin priests

Temple priests form only a small subsection of the brahmin community. The majority of those who are of the brahmin castes do not earn their livelihood from ritual practices. This is particularly the case in the West, in the diaspora communities, where temple priests are usually brought in from India. There is, however, still a certain status acquired from birth in brahmin families, even where the lifestyle adopted is not in keeping with the principles of ritual purity. It is also the case that within most Hindu communities it is still regarded as essential that the priest who performs rituals on behalf of those communities be of brahmin birth. This is changing to some extent in modern societies, albeit slowly. Some Hindu-based movements which have welcomed non-Indian converts, such as ISKCON, have been particularly effective in accelerating such changes. Nonetheless, the opinion that ritual priests must be of brahmin birth is still prevalent, particularly in India.

The priesthood and performance of ritual, moreover, is usually confined exclusively to men; any steps toward gender equality on such matters have been small and slow. Again here, certain Hindu movements have been more progressive than others. A striking example is the Gayatri Parivar, which encourages both male and female members to perform ritual worship – including the rites of *yajna*. Still, the question of women priests is not an easy one to navigate. Central issues here are firstly tradition, but secondly the notion of ritual impurity associated with menstruation. It is still the case today that most Hindu women are not encouraged to enter a temple during their period of menstruation, let alone officiating at ritual worship. Incidentally, but of particular interest to us, this is also a topic the chaplain may have to confront as many younger Hindus do not agree with what they regard as a form of discrimination based on outdated ideas of ritual purity. Within the wider Hindu society, however, the view prevails that for the ritual to yield results, it must be performed by a male brahmin priest who has been properly trained by the elders of his community.

The status of the brahmin priesthood, and the views of the wider community concerning that priesthood, is an interesting topic. The Sanskrit scriptures, including the Mahabharata and Puranas, praise the brahmins in lavish terms, and speak of the reverence, even worship, that should be devoted to them. The Mahabharata goes so far as to speak of them as being gods among men. They are the performers of ritual, but they are also depicted as the ones who give guidance to society on religious philosophy, proper conduct, and righteous living. Today, however, 'professional' brahmins tend to see their role solely as performers of ritual, or temple caretakers, and receive payment or charity for these services.

There are many Hindus today who express the view that the brahmins are interested only in money, and that they mar visits to a holy shrine with their incessant demands for payment, particularly if they see that the visitor is affluent. In addition, given the darker history of brahmins sometimes abusing their position to exploit others, many progressive Hindus today see brahmins as anachronistic, arrogant, or selfish. As a result, the respect for brahmin priests within Hindu communities has declined markedly, and it is now common to hear them spoken of disparagingly. This does not apply to all brahmins or to all members of Hindu society, but it is something one needs to be aware of. Today, Hindus generally show more respect and reverence to those they perceive as being spiritually awakened rather than merely possessing the expertise required to perform ritual. Thus sadhus, saints, and gurus, generally have higher status and more respect than the brahmin priests who perform rituals for a fee. The popularity of guru-centred movements such as ISKCON, Art of Living, and BAPS has contributed to this shift.

Ritual is common within Hindu communities, and one must be aware that such rituals are many and varied, depending upon the particular community in which they are enacted, and the region of India in which they are typically undertaken.

Ritual and modernity

We now consider the role and significance of ritual in the lives of Hindus in the modern world. Despite the changes we have discussed, Hinduism remains a religion in which ritual is important. As we have noted, ritual embodies pragmatic and devotional aspects, and in most cases it is a combination of both. In his commentaries, Shankaracharya repeatedly insists that ritual alone cannot take the soul beyond the realm of rebirth, and yet he still approves of ritual, presenting it as helpful to developing the purification essential to acquiring realised knowledge of Brahman.

In Hindu society, ritual continues to be important, although modernisation is bringing about significant changes to the religious life of many. Traditionally, ritual has been undertaken to provide help in people's journey through life; for good health, for love, for marriage, for children, for success in business, and for general well-being. Life is often precarious and people look to religion and to God for a solution to their difficulties.

Within Hindu communities in the West there is less absolute faith in supernatural solutions. To paraphrase Peter Berger: 'If I wake up in rural India and find a demon on my bed, I call for an exorcist. If I wake up in Cleveland and find a demon on my bed, I call for a psychiatrist.' One way of understanding what Berger is saying is to be aware that we live in an increasingly disenchanted world in which science provides many of the answers and solutions that religion once offered. People are less inclined to believe in supernatural forces and this leads to a declining, or at least changing, role for ritual in religious life. In the West in particular, Hindu communities are becoming less inclined to seek solutions to life's problems through ritual, and as a result changes may be required to meet the needs of communities. For instance, a Hindu parent whose child is facing a major health challenge may still sponsor a ritual to be performed at the local temple, but will likely put more energy into seeking the best medical care, and perhaps seek counselling to help cope with the stress. This is increasingly true of young Hindus, many of whom are anxious to maintain their Hindu identity but do not see ritual as the main means to achieve the goals they pursue.

That is not to say that ritual is entirely redundant in modern societies, for there is no doubt that it still has a number of important roles to play. Rites of passage are particularly significant in the life of every person from every community, and the elaborate ritual provided by Hinduism is particularly valuable for the celebration of births, marriages, funerals, and other points of transition in life. These are significant events for individuals, families, and communities, and it is thus important that they be marked in an appropriately ritualistic manner. As we will briefly discuss at the end of this section, the chaplain may play important roles in these rites.

These rituals, along with many others, play an important role in binding communities together, preserving and passing down traditions, and strengthening a sense of common identity. Many of the prayers and chants recited in the Hindu rituals are taken from the Vedas, and so must be at least 3,000 years old, and have been used for ritual purposes through the centuries by generations of Hindu priests. The famous Gayatri mantra is a very obvious example. There is something profound and emotionally potent in the recitation of a prayer that has been preserved, revered, and handed down over generations, and which is still being used by Hindus throughout the world. Such ritual practices cannot fail to strengthen the sense of community and to bind individuals together through a shared identity.

We suggested earlier that in modern societies, Hindus are less likely to seek ritual solutions to life's problems, but we must be careful not to overstate this trend. There are still times when Hindus turn to their religion for help, and surely benefit from the comfort and sense of positivity that rituals have the power to instil. Moreover, temple ritual in particular forms an important element of devotional Hinduism. Many devotees of Krishna, Rama, Durga, Vishnu, or Shiva, for instance, will attend a local temple and enact ritual worship in order to express their love and dedication toward the image of the deity. They dutifully observe the *arati* ceremonies in which items of worship and tokens of gratitude are ritually offered to God. They may also observe more elaborate ritual worship on festival days in particular. For instance, in the famous Govindaji (Krishna) temple in Jaipur, huge crowds of Hindus – young and old, wealthy and modest, educated professionals and simple labourers – throng the shrine to witness the ritual worship of the Krishna image on the altar, and verbally express their innermost devotional sentiments as they do so. Here it is clear that the rituals in such devotional ceremonies provide a sense of unity and shared belief for those who attend.

There are also tensions surrounding ritual. Some feel that over-emphasis on ritual engenders superstition and dependence on priests, and thus distracts one from aspiring toward genuine spiritual realisation. This critique is probably best summed up by the Hindu reformer and Vedantin, Swami Vivekananda, who famously stated, 'Root up priestcraft from the old religion and you get the best religion in the world' (Teachings, p161). Others may regard temple ritual as a diluting of the 'purer' Vedic rituals; the Arya Samaj movement, for instance, decries the worship of images in Hindu temples, and regards such rituals as a deviation from the Vedas. Nonetheless, the majority of contemporary Hindus recognise the importance of ritual practices as a means of preserving tradition, binding communities together, bringing comfort to those in need, and providing a means by which individuals can express their devotion to God.

We should note that ritual is not only a communal activity or something that is enacted solely by the priesthood. There is also a ritual life performed by small family groups or by individuals, and this is increasingly becoming the primary way Hindus engage with ritual. Many Hindu families have a small altar at home on which offerings are made to images of deities, which, unlike those in the temple, have not been ritually installed. This means that the offerings can be much simpler and made on an irregular basis, or even suspended during periods of absence. It is becoming more and more common for Hindu student groups at colleges and universities to mirror this more informal ritual worship on their campuses; a number of educational institutions in the West have dedicated Hindu prayer rooms for this purpose. It might even be suggested that meditation and yoga practice – performed individually or in small groups – is a form of ritual, or contains ritual elements.

ANTHROPOLOGICAL PERSPECTIVES ON HINDU RITUAL

The perspectives we have considered thus far are those of participants in ritual practice. The anthropological perspective is of the neutral observer who uses his or her training, knowledge, and expertise, to assess the significance of ritual in its social context. The anthropologist does not seek to judge the truth or otherwise of the beliefs underlying the ritual, but to understand the role of ritual within the religious systems of different societies. While it is beyond our scope here to fully represent the anthropologist's perspective, it is essential for the Hindu chaplain to recognise and understand both insider and outsider perspectives. We might also note that where anthropological studies look at religions such as Hinduism from a Western perspective, there may be some residue of the old imperialist attitudes recognisable from the early years of the discipline.

The anthropological perspective is largely based on the idea that ritual is tied to the environment in which it is enacted. Thus it will be helpful to consider the differences that exist between ritual in India's rural and urban settings, and in Hindu communities outside of India.

Hindu ritual in India

In many parts of rural India, one is likely to encounter ritual in diverse, localised forms that will not be encountered elsewhere. These are often conducted along caste lines, and may demand the participation of brahmin priests. While such customs and rituals are of interest to the anthropologist, their highly localised nature makes it difficult to apply any generalised understanding gleaned from their study to Hinduism as a whole. One might classify some of these folk- or village-based practices under the heading of magic as much as religion, and some involve the worship of nature spirits, demons, or even ghosts, in a way that seems quite removed from what has come to be recognised as mainstream Hinduism.

From an anthropological perspective, one might suggest that rituals of this type belong to pre-modern societies, and will tend to disappear amongst Hindu communities living in urban India or in the West. This certainly does appear to be the case, particularly amongst the younger generations, and one will often hear sceptical views expressed with regard to such practices. Moreover, there is perhaps a fear that any emphasis on such folk practices undermines the status of Hinduism as a world religion, and hence, where they do persist, there is a tendency to avoid revealing their presence to outsiders. Nonetheless, these folk or village customs must not be entirely ignored or discounted as they have to some degree transferred themselves to urban India and can still be encountered amongst diaspora communities, although predominantly amidst the older generations.

The experience of one British Hindu is revealing here. While living at home in Britain, he regarded village ritual as 'stuff and nonsense', but when he returned to India, particularly when he stayed in his family's home village for weeks or months, he began to feel that it was probably best not to take the chance of ignoring the old folk rituals, and potentially angering the spirits who were the object of worship. Here we can see how context can affect attitudes and patterns of belief regarding ritual acts.

When anthropologists turn their attention to the high importance of ritual in the Hindu tradition, they must acknowledge its close connection with the social and political status of the Brahmin caste. Traditionally, Hindu India was ruled by an occasionally uneasy alliance of brahmins with the *kshatriyas* – the royal families of the Indian states. Some of these kings were immensely powerful, and used their wealth to build and endow the temples on which brahmins depended for livelihood. The temple in turn was not only a place of worship, but a centre for social and economic activity. Of course, the rituals had to be enacted in the proper way, but this was just one of the activities for which the priests took responsibility. The Muslim conquests largely destroyed this system in North and Central India, as the Hindu monarchies were replaced by the Delhi Sultanate and then the Mogul Empire. This political transformation coincided with, and in part led to, the introduction of rituals of a different kind – less brahminical and more popular in nature.

Most of the old temples were renovated and reopened under British rule, but the previous status of the temple communities was never restored. In South India, which remained largely under Hindu rule, the traditional role of the temple was retained. Hindu emperors expanded the size of the buildings in which the ritual was performed, and gave substantial economic support to the large brahmin communities that grew around them. These endowments often took the form of land and villages, and in this way the ritual life of Hindu India was closely linked to the social and economic systems. Some large temples supported communities of several thousand brahmins, and for this reason alone high levels of income were essential.

India's independence in 1947 brought about dramatic changes in the position of the temples and the brahmins who officiated over them. The Constitution of the Indian Republic is secular and hence state support for religious rituals ended. Even under British rule, Hindu princes had continued to provide economic largesse for temples and brahmins, but independence put an end to this situation in most cases. Today the rituals are conducted independently of the government, and the upkeep of the temples and the livelihood of the priests depend on individual donations or fees paid for services.

In addition, recent decades have witnessed increasing opposition to the social status of brahmins from Hindu reform groups and left-wing political parties. The results of these changes are less able to claim exclusive status or exclude members of lower castes from participating in rituals, although this is less so in parts of rural India. As we touched upon earlier, the general perception of the priests has changed as they are frequently regarded as employees dependent upon the wealth of others, rather than as the natural leaders of society. From the perspective of the brahmin communities, it has become increasingly difficult to maintain a livelihood based exclusively on temple and priestly ritual.

This financial pressure has been augmented by the fact that improved healthcare in India and lower infant mortality rates mean that the family groups dependent upon temple income have tended to grow larger. As a result, many brahmins have now been forced to take up other professions alongside their ritual services, and many have abandoned the priestly profession entirely. It is in this situation, that brahmins have acquired something of a reputation for being avaricious and concerned primarily with financial gain; from an anthropological perspective, however, one can see how social and economic changes in India have led to this somewhat worldly approach to ritual life. It is also the case that many brahmins remain deeply committed to their religion, to serving their communities, and to the preservation of ancient traditions that they hold dear. The loss of such communities and the knowledge they possess would therefore be a tragedy for the Hindu community as a whole, and thus there are arguments in support for the priestly lifestyle.

Hindu ritual in the diaspora

When we turn to diaspora communities, the anthropological perspective on ritual highlights the tension between preservation and adaptation. In the aftermath of mass migration, diaspora communities face numerous challenges, among which the need for economic security and the desire to preserve religion, culture, and tradition, are notable. These aspirations may often be in conflict, as those who rigidly insist on living according to tradition and religious custom may find that these present barriers to economic progress. The education and status of women is one obvious example.

As a rule, Hindu communities have shown themselves to be willing to change, adapt, and even abandon traditional practices in order to integrate and thereby prosper in their new environments. For instance, traditions such as arranged marriages and the rigid observance of caste rules are in decline, as younger generations aspire toward a more Western lifestyle. This is a significant sociological trend amongst diaspora communities, and one might wonder whether there will be much to distinguish Western Hindus from the wider community in another two or three generations. Ritual may be a deciding factor.

It is impossible to exactly predict the effect of rapid cultural change on the ritual life of diaspora Hinduism, but it seems clear that significant transformations are underway. In Hindu communities in the West, there is little doubt that the old rituals are mostly seen as no longer suitable in their most orthodox forms, and that changes will have to be made in order to meet the needs of communities that have become significantly westernised. As we have noted, Hindus are becoming less inclined to look to ritual as a primary solution to the problems of life, in part because scientific and medical solutions are increasingly available, and in part because of a declining level of belief in the efficacy of ritual. Moreover, the extensive recitation of Sanskrit prayer, which mostly cannot be understood by those observing the ritual, makes participation increasingly less attractive for those seeking a meaningful experience. It may be that we will see a move toward shortened forms of ritual and increased use of vernacular languages, including English and European languages.

Indeed, it is becoming increasingly common to find rituals adapted to also serve as an educational experience for those in attendance. Many Hindus will now include pauses in the ritual's liturgical flow to allow for translations of the prayers and explanations of the meaning and function of the ritual. It seems, anecdotally at least, that there has been a positive response from diaspora communities where such innovations have been introduced. As we will touch on in the conclusion of the section, this may also be an area for the chaplain to engage with ritual – either as the performer of such modified rituals, or as a 'translator', particularly where the ritual priests have only limited skills in local languages, or where they do not fully understand the meaning of the rituals they enact.

The disenchantment of the modern world referred to earlier does not necessarily mean that temple worship and ritual in general is likely to lose its place at the heart of the Hindu religious life. To the contrary, attendance at temples, and even the building of new temples, seem to be on the rise in the diaspora. In India and the West, one can observe that despite, or perhaps because of, rapid modernisation, attendance at the large temples is increasing. Amongst diaspora communities, we can also observe new and more grandiose temples being opened every year and priests being imported from India to ensure that the rituals are performed in the proper manner.

Further study is needed to fully explain this phenomenon, but we can articulate a few key factors. One reason may be the rise of a wealthy middle class who look to the temple as the hub of festivals and social events so that religious life is combined with leisure and social interaction.

A second factor to consider is the role that temple ritual plays in forming a sense of identity. Despite the pronounced trend toward integration with the wider community, there remains a desire to preserve a Hindu identity among members of the diaspora, and the temples provide a focal point for that. As we have noted, diaspora Hindus tend to be averse to what they regard as overly elaborate and incomprehensible rituals; nevertheless, most also believe that such ceremonies are an essential means of preserving a Hindu identity in the West.

Another factor is that temples have evolved beyond their ritual purpose. Today temples are used for a variety of functions, and are often better regarded as community centres rather than solely as places of worship. These hybrid temple–community-centres provide a focus for secular activities in an environment steeped in ritual. The installation of sacred images and the ritual worship offered to them remain central, but the temple fulfils a wider range of other functions that preserve a sense of community and identity. It is not uncommon, for instance, for Hindu families to engage in worship while bringing their children to academic tutoring or music classes held at the temple, or for temples to host youth camps which combine ritual, academic, cultural, and athletic activities.

A final factor to take into account is the power of devotional sentiments. Within Western diaspora communities, as in India, temple ritual and temple visits form an integral part of the worship for the forms of devotional Hinduism that remain such a prominent feature of the tradition. This is especially the case with regard to temples affiliated with particular movements or gurus. Thus, we might particularly note the ISKCON temples dedicated to Krishna, or those of the Swaminarayan community – often built on an elaborate scale like that in Neasden, North London. For the adherents of these movements, engaging in ritual at their temples is central to their spiritual practice. Other Hindus, who may not feel the same affiliation, might attend more infrequently or only for major holidays. Yet even these more casual congregants often express admiration for the devotional mood they find in these temples and in the rituals they observe.

In discussing the Hindu diaspora's relationship to ritual, we have focused on temple ritual. However, we must also consider the continuing demand for ritual ceremonies marking rites of passage. These include weddings, funerals, and pre-natal blessing ceremonies, among others. Hindu weddings in particular continue to be large affairs at which families and friends congregate to celebrate the union of two families. Weddings form such an important part of Hindu culture that it is quite common for even non-religious Hindus to opt for the elaborate and authentic form of the ritual to mark such an event. As we have mentioned earlier, in many cases innovations have been introduced, with pauses and translations inserted at various junctures in the proceedings so that the significance of each part of the ritual can be explained to the congregation. Weddings of this type are becoming increasingly popular, particularly in cases of interfaith or interracial unions, and it may well be that this is a trend that will become more pronounced.

Drawing from this overview of the anthropological perspective, we can observe that social modernisation in India and the formation of diaspora communities in the West has changed Hindu engagement with ritual. On the one hand, modernisation does inevitably lead to a less 'enchanted' world view, which means in turn that modern Hindus place less faith in the primacy of ritual solutions to life's challenges. Moreover, the change in the economic status of the brahmin castes has led to significant changes in attitude in the wider community, and inevitably some decline in the respect felt for the priests who perform ritual. On the other hand, we must also be aware of an ongoing demand for ritual, albeit with certain significant changes and adaptations. The growth of the diaspora and of a newly-empowered middle class in India has led to a greater focus on temples as centres of community life and social interaction and has fuelled renewed interest in ritual as a means of fostering identity and observing rites of passage.

Hence, the conclusion we may draw from our donning the hat of the anthropologist is that while orthodox forms of ritual might be under threat in diaspora communities, for a number of different reasons it seems likely that ritual itself will continue to play a significant role in the cultural and social lives of most Hindus. There is, moreover, an openness to change, and in particular a demand for the rituals to be explained rather than simply being enacted in front of a congregation that is little more than a passive audience. It is likely that vernacular languages will come to play an increasing role in the performance of ritual, particularly in terms of providing an explanation of the ritual that is comprehensible by younger generations, even while there remains a profound reverence for the Sanskrit language and the enunciation of the Vedic hymns.

CONCLUSION: THE HINDU CHAPLAIN AND RITUAL

From our brief exploration of Hinduism and ritual – seen through the historical, anthropological, and practitioner lenses – we can appreciate how complex and dynamic this relationship is. It is clear that ritual remains central to Hinduism and must not be ignored. What is the Hindu chaplain's role in this? A Hindu chaplain might engage with ritual in a number of ways based on several factors, including his or her own background and comfort level, the expectations of the community members being ministered to, and the context. To conclude this session, we touch on a few different modes of engagement.

One scenario we might consider is that of the Hindu chaplain who does not directly engage with ritual. This may be due to the chaplain not coming from a Hindu background or not feeling comfortable with the rituals. Female chaplains serving in more orthodox Hindu communities may also feel reluctant to directly engage with ritual for reasons we have already discussed. In such a scenario, chaplains might simply connect members of the community with ritual priests when the need arises. Even then the chaplain would have to be sensitive to the ritual needs of the community and familiar enough with them to help connect them to appropriate resources. Moreover, he or she might have to act as a go-between to ensure that the community members and the priest understand and are comfortable with one another. Such a chaplain might best be described as a coordinator or facilitator of ritual.

A Hindu chaplain who does not directly engage with ritual at all is quite rare; a more common scenario would be for the chaplain to connect community members with ritual priests but to also participate in the ritual as an educator and 'translator' alongside the ritual priest. Such a chaplain should become familiar with the range of rituals performed by the priests and acquire an understanding of their meaning, so as to explain them to the community when needed. It has become increasingly common, for instance, to see Hindu chaplains at weddings and funerals, seated alongside the ritual priest and explaining the rituals.

A third scenario to consider: the Hindu chaplain might officiate over some rituals, particularly those connected to devotional worship or festival celebrations. As discussed earlier, ritual in contemporary Hinduism has largely shifted away from the Vedic rites and more toward temple- and family-based celebrations. Chaplains might thus feel comfortable engaging with such rituals by analogising their roles to those of family members rather than to orthodox brahmins. This might be a particularly helpful approach for chaplains coming from non-brahmin backgrounds or for female chaplains. These chaplains might not feel comfortable officiating at other rituals, however, especially when such rituals are more complex, draw more from the earlier Vedic tradition, or explicitly call for brahmins to oversee them. In those cases, the chaplain would likely still connect the community to a trained priest and perform the supplementary role of offering explanations that we discussed earlier.

A fourth and related scenario might involve a chaplain learning how to officiate over rituals for his or her community members. This would require the chaplain to find an educational institution that is equipped and willing to teach ritual practice. Since ritual priests traditionally come from families of priests and are taught from childhood, few orthodox schools are set up to facilitate adult education, and some may be reluctant to accept candidates from non-brahmin backgrounds. Still, chaplains who are interested in learning ritual may find opportunities through newer Hindu groups or reform movements – the Gayatri Parivar and ISKCON, for instance, both offer some resources. The internet might also help chaplains to connect with resources and opportunities for non-traditional study of ritual.

One chaplain's experience illustrates this scenario:

> I was born and raised in the United States as a child of non-brahmin immigrants (my family is from a sub-caste within the Kshatriya community). As a full-time Hindu chaplain at a university, I came to appreciate the importance of helping community members – particularly those of the younger generations – with their ritual needs. I therefore embarked on formal and informal study of ritual with teachers from the Chaitanya Vaishnava and Sri Vaishnava lineages, Hindu traditions that tend to adopt a more liberal stance on the eligibility of non-brahmins to officiate ritual. As a result, I have been asked to officiate over rites, including weddings, by members

> of the community who are looking for ceremonies that emphasise the meaning of the ritual over the technicalities. For example, two alumni of the university asked me to officiate their Hindu wedding at the university chapel, and requested me to design a ceremony that honours the tradition, but also contains elements of a modern western wedding and would be comprehensible to both their Hindu and non-Hindu guests. On the other hand, for members of the community who prefer a more traditional or caste-specific approach, I am able to offer help in other ways. For example, a former student who is now engaged, and who hails from a Tamil brahmin background, recently asked for my help to connect her family with an orthodox brahmin priest from that community who would also be open to having me assist in explaining the rituals.

A fifth scenario, however rare it might currently be, is that of a ritual priest, trained from an early age, called to enter the field of chaplaincy in the diaspora. As we have discussed, Hindu temples generally bring ritual priests over from India to tend to temple worship and to officiate over Sanskrit rituals for the community. Most of these priests will not be equipped with the tools necessary to minister to the congregation's other needs, what to speak of being educated in any form of counselling or pastoral care. In fact, few of these priests will even have the proficiency in the languages of their host countries needed to meaningfully interact with many of their community members. Still, it may happen that as the diaspora grows and the needs of congregations grow with it, temple managers and brahmin communities begin to recognise the benefits of offering ritual priests additional training to equip some of them to serve as chaplains. Younger priests may especially find this a fulfilling vocation and a natural extension of their religious education. Such priests will, in many ways, face the opposite challenge to that we have discussed with the other scenarios. They will have the expertise in ritual, but must learn to adapt and adjust the ritual to meet the pastoral needs of the community.

4. APPLIED HINDU ETHICS

The main focus for this section is the vexed question of Hindu ethics and the ways in which ideas on ethics can shape and influence the chaplain's work. Although the main emphasis here is on morality, and moral ambiguity, we will also draw in issues of guilt, grief, and tragedy, and ways of confronting the discomfort that life throws at us from time to time. Questions of ethics are an essential feature of most religious traditions, and it is common to find religions offering clear-cut codes of conduct that adherents are expected to follow. Hinduism does not quite follow this pattern, and the ambiguity that Hindu teachings present is one of the main issues that Hindu chaplains will confront.

HINDU VIEWS ON MORAL AMBIGUITY IN DECISION-MAKING

It is true to say that virtually all religions act as some form of authority over the lives and thoughts of adherents. The location of that authority, however, varies considerably between faiths, and it is important to be aware of these variations. At the risk of oversimplification, one might say that religious authority is to be found in sacred text, in the institution, in charismatic leaders, in family and community, and perhaps in individual inspiration as well. Most religions provide more than one source of authority, but overall it is possible to recognise the area in which moral authority is most typically found.

In Islam, for example, sacred text in the form of the Qur'an, and the works of Sharia, are the most significant sources of authority, whilst for Christianity authority lies in the Bible but also in its institutions.

When we turn to consider the location of authority in Hinduism, we will see that all of these potential sources are relevant, and need to be taken into consideration. If we look firstly at sacred text, seeking out a 'Hindu Sharia', then immediately problems arise. It is certainly the case that texts such as the Ramayana, Bhagavad-gita, and Mahabharata, are regarded with reverence within Hindu communities, but these are not works that are dedicated specifically to providing rules of life. They do present forms of moral guidance, but they do not offer clear rules that Hindus are obliged to follow. It is also the case that the general Hindu attitude to sacred text is different to that encountered within Islam or Christianity. It is quite rare for a scripture to be studied word for word, and, moreover, such texts are regarded as sources of guidance rather than as absolute authority.

There are ancient Sanskrit texts that give precise rules of conduct but it is important that we understand their role and status within the Hindu traditions. These texts are known as *smritis*, or *dharma-shastras*, and the best known of these are probably the Manu Smriti, the Yajñavalkya Smriti, and the Vishnu Smriti. These works are sometimes cited by followers of other religions and by scholars when they refer to Hindu ethics, but few Hindus know these texts well.

A problem with the *smritis* is that they contain injunctions, particularly in relation to caste and gender, which today are unacceptable or irrelevant to most Hindus. Here are a few examples.

> Kshattris, Ugras, and Pukkasas, live by trapping animals that live in holes in the ground. Dhigvanas are leather workers, Venas play drums.

> These people must live near well-known trees or burial grounds. They must make themselves known by special marks, and live by their designated occupations.
>
> However, the dwellings of Chandalas and Svapakkas must be outside the village. They are Apapatras who are not allowed to use the same vessels and pots, and their wealth consists of dogs and donkeys. (Manu Smriti, 10.47–51)

> In childhood a female must be subject to her father, in youth to her husband, and when her lord is dead to her sons; a woman must never be independent.
>
> She must not seek to separate herself from her father, husband, or sons; by leaving them, she would make both families contemptible.
>
> She must always be cheerful, clever in the management of household affairs, careful in cleaning her utensils, and economical in her expenditure.
>
> He to whom her father may give her, or her brother with her father's permission, she must obey as long as he lives, and when he is dead she must not insult his memory.
>
> Though destitute of virtue, seeking pleasure elsewhere, or devoid of good qualities, a husband must always be worshipped as a god by a faithful wife. (Manu Smriti, 5.148–54)

These are admittedly extreme examples of the type of material encountered in the *smriti* texts, but they do demonstrate the difficulties that would arise if they were still to be referred to as Hindu law. If confronted with material of this type, many Hindus will say that they may have been applicable in ancient times, but are not relevant for today.

So let us consider the other potential sources of authority. Religious institutions and their leaders can often provide significant authority in moral issues, but, as we have noted,

Hinduism is a largely non-institutional tradition. There are, however, numerous sects that are hierarchical and structured, though with varying degrees of rigour and acceptance. Members of these groups may regard the leadership as a significant source of moral authority, though we must be aware that this would apply only to a relatively small minority of Hindus. The Gujarati Swaminarayan sect, now prominent in the West, serves as a useful example here. For members of this group, the leadership provides clear moral guidance, and young people in particular are often giving counselling sessions, particularly if they are deemed by their parents to be 'going off the rails'. Moreover, the recorded words and writings of the founder, Swaminarayan himself, are also taken as authoritative on many issues of conduct and lifestyle.

As this institutional form of moral authority applies to only a minority of Hindus, others may seek the guidance of gurus or sadhus who do not hold a position in any formal institution but are identified as charismatic leaders with higher knowledge and spiritual insights. Again, this authority will apply only to those individuals who have accepted such a person as their teacher and guide, and the opinions each of them expresses cannot be regarded as a definitive Hindu ethics.

Traditionally, and to a large extent still today, the main source of authority for many Hindus has been family and community. This means that ethical standards will vary considerably between different communities, and between different families. A Hindu asked why he or she strictly adhered to a vegetarian diet might reply: 'Because my mother told me I should be vegetarian.' In Hindu society, caste has for centuries played a significant role, socially and economically, and caste leaders held the power and authority to insist on a lifestyle that was seen as appropriate for their community. This meant that an individual risked social and economic ostracism if he or she deviated from the ethical standards insisted upon by the caste leadership. Even Mahatma Gandhi was expelled from his caste for crossing the sea to study abroad, and in the Brahmavaivarta

Purana we find Radha being warned by a friend that she will lose her caste status due to her illicit love affair with Krishna (Sri Krishna Janma Khand, 94.19).

Today, however, with urbanisation, migration, and social change, the hold that caste exerts over individuals is diminishing. In the West in particular, and especially among young Hindus, caste identity is of much less significance than in the past, and the elders of the community are less able to enforce ethical standards. Many Hindus, young and old, now believe that caste does more harm than good, and that the move away from caste identity is a positive trend in Hinduism. Families, nuclear and extended, can still exert influence over their members' conduct, but even here that influence is declining, not least because highly educated individuals are less likely to be economically dependent on family ties. Most Hindus still display a great deal of respect for parents and the elders of the family, but they may be less inclined to adhere to a lifestyle that is often seen as outdated and overly rooted in Indian culture.

If caste, community, and family, are becoming less significant sources of moral authority, does this mean that Hindus living in modern society are without rules or moral constraints of any type? While it seems increasingly the case that there are no formal sets of rules that all Hindus will be expected to abide by, at the same time wider teachings on dharma give key precepts by which righteous persons will be expected to live. These are not rules as such, and it is up to the individual to determine how best to implement them in any given situation. What we are talking about here are ideals such as not harming (*ahimsa*), honesty, charity, kindness, respect, integrity, and concern for the welfare of all living beings. There are no specific rules, no Sharia, dictating precisely how these moral precepts are to be implemented, but they remain central to the notion of Sanatana Dharma, which in turn can be regarded as the essence of the Hindu religious tradition. For many Hindus, living in accordance with such principles forms a part of their devotion to God, but it is also the case that dharma stands independently, with or without reference to any deity or the worship of that deity. Even a Hindu who is an atheist should still abide by the precepts of Sanatana Dharma.

Although this idea of a fluid sense of morality closely reflects the ethos of modernity, we should not think that it is an idea that is exclusively modern. Here is an account from the Mahabharata of instruction given by Krishna to Arjuna. The passage is from the Karna Parvan (Book 8), which tells of the fighting that took place at Kurukshetra after the fall of Bhishma and Drona. Karna is made the commander of the Kaurava host, and we hear of the bitter fighting that took place as he led the army into battle against the Pandavas. Whilst Arjuna is distracted on another part of the field, Karna focuses his attention on Yudhishthira, and severely wounds him with his arrows. Without anyone to protect him, Yudhishthira is forced to run from the field before Karna, and is left in a state of mental and physical torment. When Arjuna eventually comes to assist his elder brother it is too late, and Yudhishthira condemns Arjuna, and says that he might as well give up the bow named Gandiva and let another, more valiant, warrior bear it. These words of Yudhishthira are unjust to Arjuna, but the situation is made even worse when Arjuna reveals that he has vowed to behead anyone who says that he should give up the Gandiva bow. For Arjuna a vow can never be broken, and so he draws his sword to strike down Yudhishthira.

It is at this point that Krishna intervenes:

Karna Parvan (Book 8), Chapter 49

> [Krishna said to Arjuna] Stop! Stop! No one who understands the distinctions of dharma would ever act in such a way. You do not know about the decisions made by learned men who teach disciples about matters of right conduct. It is never easy to

determine what course of action should be followed and what should be avoided, but it is possible if one follows the guidance of scripture. You think that you know what dharma is, but by acting in this way as if it were dharma you are showing your ignorance of dharma for the killing of a living being is forbidden by those who truly adhere to dharma. In my opinion, never killing any living being is the highest dharma; one may speak a falsehood but one should never kill another being. So how is it that you are prepared to kill the king, your elder brother who is himself one who comprehends dharma? The vow you took was an act of folly and now as another act of folly you are preparing to embrace *adharma*. Why are you going to do this without thinking properly about dharma? The true end of dharma is certainly a subtle matter, which is hard to understand.

Now listen to a narration which reflects on the subtle and complex nature of dharma. One who speaks the truth adheres to dharma; there is no virtue higher than truthfulness. However, the practice of the essence of truth can be very difficult to comprehend. There are a number of occasions on which one may speak a lie: at a marriage, to woo a woman, when one's life or property is threatened and for the sake of a brahmin. On such occasions falsehood becomes truth and truth becomes falsehood. Anyone who adheres blindly to the principle of speaking the truth is no better than a fool.

There was a sadhu named Kausika who was not well-read in the teachings on dharma. He lived a good distance from any village, at a place where a number of rivers met, and he had taken the following vow: 'I must always speak the truth.' He became famous for his adherence to this principle. Once some people came to the forest where he

> lived attempting to escape with their possessions from a gang of ferocious robbers. The robbers then approached Kausika and said, 'A host of people came by here a little while ago. Which way did they go?' Kausika told the truth, 'They entered this wood here.' Acting on this information, the robbers pursued their victims and when they found them they killed them all. And because of the *adharma* of speaking the truth, Kausika was reborn in a low state of life.
>
> There has to be some way of distinguishing dharma. Some say the highest knowledge is gained through reason (*tarka*) but many others say one gains knowledge of dharma from the *shruti* (scriptures). I do not disagree with this, but the *shruti* does not refer to every individual case. Dharma was created for the welfare of living beings, and hence whatever sustains living beings is dharma. So we must understand dharma as that which leads to the welfare of people in the world. Now that I have given you a clear definition of dharma you must decide whether Yudhishthira should be slaughtered.

Arjuna accepts Krishna's guidance, but asks if there is some way of getting out of this dilemma without breaking his vow. Krishna then suggests that as an insult is often said to be equal to death he might 'kill' his elder brother with insulting words, thereby escaping from an impossible predicament. Arjuna accepts this advice, and the problem is resolved.

The significant point is that Krishna refuses to accept the view that morality can be defined by a set of rules that must be followed in all circumstances. The obvious fact is that each case is different, and, as the story of Kausika illustrates, there may be times when it is wrong to follow a rule. The final paragraph is particularly interesting. Here Krishna defines dharma as that which brings about the welfare of other living beings; it is up to Arjuna to decide how this is to be applied. This view of morality, expressed by Krishna in an ancient Sanskrit text, remains the predominant Hindu perspective in the modern world.

In one sense, this approach to ethics seems enlightened and eminently reasonable, but it could also lead to confusion and a lack of direction. It may seem that Hinduism has no proper rules at all, and that everyone is free to do whatever they like. Questions of an ethical nature related to alcohol, diet, contraception, abortion, marriage, and divorce, receive no direct answers, and for some this is problematic and inappropriate for one of the world's major religions. People often want clear answers to moral questions, and whilst complex moral arguments may be more rational, they do not satisfy the natural requirement for clarity and simplicity. Again we must emphasise that where individuals attach themselves to a particular authority – a religious group or teacher – then those straightforward answers will often be forthcoming, but for the most Hindus this is not the case, particularly where the authority of caste and family is in decline.

What Hinduism does have is firm values and principles, and this is a point we have sought to emphasise. These do not today amount to a clearly asserted set of incontrovertible rules, for, as Krishna pointed out, rules do not work for every time and place, and can lead to the perpetration of various forms of immorality. Moreover, the precepts and values presented as a definition of Sanatana Dharma do constitute a powerful moral force that must be taken seriously, even though one may not be able to apply them at all times. Human beings are generally imperfect, but the precepts of Sanatana Dharma give a clear statement of the values one must consistently strive to implement in life. This requires intelligence, sound advice, integrity, and the acceptance of one's own limitations and shortcomings, but from an objective perspective we can observe that it offers a genuinely viable approach to the vexed question of human morality.

Here are a few of the many statements from ancient texts in which the values of Sanatana Dharma are set out.

adrohah sarva-bhuteshu
karmana manasa gira
anugrahas cha danam cha
satam dharmah sanatanah

Never displaying malice towards any living being through actions, thoughts, or words; acts of kindness; and giving in charity. This is the Sanatana Dharma adhered to by righteous persons. (Mahabharata 3.281.34)

ahimsa satyam akrodho
danam etac chatushtayam
ajata-shatro sevasva
dharma esha sanatanah

Not harming, truthfulness, remaining free from anger, and charity, are the four practices you must adhere to, Ajatashatru. This is the Sanatana Dharma. (Mahabharata 13.147.22)

dushkaram parama-jnanam
tarkenatra vyavasyati
shrutir dharma iti hy eke
vadanti bahavo janah

na tv etat parisuyami
na hi sarvam vidhiyate
prabhavarthaya bhutanam
dharma-pravachanam kritam

dharanad dharmam ity ahur
dharmo dharayati prajah

yah syad dharana-samyuktah
sa dharma iti nischayah

The superior understanding is hard to achieve, but one may be able to reach a determination on the basis of logic. Many persons, however, assert that it is *shruti* (scripture) that defines dharma.

I do not reject this point of view, but not every case can be resolved in this way. The precepts of dharma have been set in place in order to allow living beings to flourish.

Hence people conclude that dharma is based on the principle of sustenance, for dharma sustains living beings. Whatever may bring about the sustenance of living beings is therefore dharma; this must be the conclusion. (Mahabharata 8.49.48–50)

sri bhagavan uvacha
abhayam sattva-samshuddhir
jñana-yoga-vyavasthitih
danam damas cha
yajñas cha svadhyayas tapa arjavam

ahimsa satyam akrodhas
tyagah shantir apaishunam
daya bhuteshv aloluptvam
mardavam hrir achapalam

tejah kshama dhritih shaucham
adroho natimanita
bhavanti sampadam daivim
abhijatasya bharata

Fearlessness, being pure in heart, remaining resolute in the pursuit of knowledge through yoga practice, charity, self-control, performing sacrifices, reciting the Vedas, austerity, honesty, Not harming, truthfulness, avoiding anger, renunciation, tranquillity, never maligning others, compassion for other beings, remaining free from greed; kindness, modesty, never wavering, energy, patience, resolve, purity, the absence of malice and of arrogance; these constitute the qualities of one born with the godly disposition, Bharata. (Bhagavad-gita 16.1–3).

sarvam priyabhyupagatam
dharmam ahur manishinah
pashyaitam lakshanad desham
dharmadharme yudhishthira

The wise say that dharma is whatever is based on love for all beings. This is the characteristic mark that distinguishes dharma from its antithesis (*adharma*), Yudhisthira. (Mahabharata 12.251.24).

anukrosho hi sadhunam
su-mahad-dharma-lakshanam
anukroshas cha sadhunam
sada pritim prayacchati

For righteous persons, compassion is the great characteristic mark of dharma; and compassion is always a source of delight for the righteous. (Mahabharata 13.5.23).

yada chayam na bibheti
yada chasman na bibhyeti
yada nechhati na dveshti
tada sidhyati vai dvijah

yada na kurute bhavam
sarva-bhuteshu papakam

karmana manasa vacha
brahma sampadyate tada

When a brahmin no longer has any fear, when no fear arises because of him, and when he feels neither desire nor loathing, he has certainly achieved success.

When he is never the cause of any harmful condition for any living being with his actions, thoughts, or words, then he has achieved Brahman. (Mahabharata 12.254.16–17)

adrohenaiva bhutanam
alpa-drohena va punah
ya vrittih sa paro-dharmas
tena jivami jajale

Causing no harm to any living being, or at least as little harm as possible, is the way of life that represents the highest expression of dharma. That is the rule by which I live, Jajali. (Mahabharata 12.254.6)

ata urdhvam pravakshyami
niyatam dharma-lakshanam
ahimsa lakshano dharmo
himsa chadharma-lakshana

Now then I will speak about what is accepted as the characteristic mark of dharma. *Ahimsa* (not-harming) is the characteristic mark of dharma, whilst *himsa* (harming) is the characteristic mark of its antithesis, *adharma*. (Mahabharata)

The chaplain might well be advised to undertake a more detailed study of works such as the Mahabharata, Ramayana, Bhagavad-gita, and Bhagavata Purana, in order to gain a deeper insight. Later we will look in some greater detail at the ideas embodied in the Mahabharata and Ramayana, but the main point to emphasise here is the importance of establishing the key precepts that must be applied in the pursuit of the ideal Hindu way of life.

In the chaplain's work, questions relating to diet, alcohol, abortion, sexuality, and other such ethical issues, will arise. In discussing such issues, it is important, as far as possible, to avoid dogmatic assertions, and to maintain an emphasis on the precepts considered above. Each situation is different and conclusions to ethical dilemmas can best be arrived through discussion with an emphasis on the central values of Sanatana Dharma. Where morality is approached in this way, with less emphasis on set rules, there is always the possibility that persons may delude themselves into thinking that what they want to do is what is right, and this is where intelligence and integrity come to the fore. Above all, the Hindu dharma demands sincerity from its followers, and a genuine desire to do what is right rather than what is convenient or pleasurable. The Hindu chaplain must explore these issues with sensitivity and concern in order to help those he or she will come to serve.

Exercise

1. Explain the issue of moral ambiguity in relation to the Hindu religious tradition. How does this affect the work of the Hindu chaplain?

THE APPLICATION OF HINDU ETHICS IN PROFESSIONAL SETTINGS

The values we have considered above, the central values of Sanatana Dharma, can be applied to a range of professional settings, and arguably in every walk of life. They are not just rules to live by but fundamental characteristics that shape the type of person we become, and this should be evident wherever our lives may lead us. Compassion, kindness, tolerance, and the commitment to help others, form the essence of Hindu dharma, and these precepts are applicable at some stage in all professions, not least in the manner in which we conduct ourselves in relation to others.

Universal compassion and dedication to others' welfare are clearly essential qualities for health professionals, but one might question whether such values are applicable to the military, or whether it is possible for those engaged in business or politics to be absolutely honest at all times and display no hostility towards others. Some have even argued that the emphasis on such values makes Hindu communities weak and open to subjection by others. At this point, it seems pertinent to consider in more detail the ideals of karma-yoga, which receive particular emphasis in the opening chapters of the Bhagavad-gita.

The Bhagavad-gita is a passage of the Mahabharata, and appears just before the final conflict at Kurukshetra is about to take place. Here we find Arjuna, the greatest warrior of the Pandava host, suddenly becoming overcome with doubts and misgivings, firstly over whether the waging of war against family members is in accordance with dharma, and secondly over whether it will be possible for them to enjoy the spoils of victory after engaging in such a ghastly course of action. It is in response to such doubts that Krishna, an earthly manifestation of the supreme deity, delivers the discourse known as the Bhagavad-gita, which forms eighteen chapters of the sixth book of the Mahabharata.

Krishna's initial response (Chapter 2) is to chide Arjuna for weakness of resolve, but he moves on quickly to insist on the immortality of the soul, pointing out that death is never the end of a living being. It is around the middle of Chapter 2 that the text moves on to introduce the idea of karma-yoga as a means of resolving Arjuna's dilemma, and relieving him of the grief that has overcome him. In 2.47 we find these words that introduce the concept:

karmany evadhikaras te
ma phaleshu kadachana
ma karma-phala-hetur bhur
ma te sango 'stv akarmani

> You have a right to perform prescribed action, but you are not entitled to the fruits of that action. Do not make the rewards of action your motive, and do not develop any attachment for avoiding action. (Bhagavad-gita 2.47)

The idea is that work must be performed out of a sense of duty, and should not be motivated by aspirations for material gain. Family, community, and society as a whole have a need for everyone to work diligently for the good of all, and it is this sense of personal sacrifice that epitomises the notion of karma-yoga. The emphasis here is primarily on motivation. The ideal person acts out of duty, self-abnegation, and a desire to promote the welfare of all beings, and the state of consciousness that underpins this selfless approach is one that is regarded as profoundly spiritual; hence it is designated as a form of yoga, the yoga of action. The point is that in order to fully develop this renounced approach to work and action, one needs to move toward a state of consciousness that is more preoccupied with the soul, the true self, than with the world and worldly gain. This may be based on realisation of one's own spiritual identity, or as an expression of devotion to God, both are referred to in the Gita, but in either case we can see how desireless action is seen as a form of spiritual progress.

It is not the case, however, that any action performed without selfish motive can be included under the heading of karma-yoga. The action must be in accordance with the precepts of dharma, and it must therefore be performed in a way that brings about the welfare of other living beings. This is made clear in the third chapter:

karmanaiva hi samsiddhim
asthita janakadayah
loka-samgraham evapi
sampashyan kartum arhasi

> It was through the performance of action alone that Janaka and other kings attained a state of complete perfection. Just by considering the welfare of the world, you should be inspired to act (Bhagavad-gita 3.20)

King Janaka is cited by Krishna as a perfect performer of the karma-yoga, and, as the second line makes clear, his actions were performed solely for the welfare of others. Moreover:

yad yad acharati sresthas
tat tad evetaro janah
sa yat pramanam kurute
lokas tad anuvartate

> Whatever course of action a superior man pursues, lesser persons will follow, and the world accepts the standard he sets. (Bhagavad-gita 3.21)

So not only does the ideal of karma-yoga dictate that one should act without desire, for the welfare of the world, but also in a manner that provides an example for others to follow. Hence we can conclude that these opening chapters of the Bhagavad-gita instruct that ideally action should be performed without selfish motivation, for the good of all, and in a manner that provides a perfect example of good conduct. Of course, we cannot expect that all people, or even a large number of people, will be able to adopt the perfect standard that Krishna appears to demand, but what is given here is an ideal towards which we may aspire, even if it is only gradually, and only to some limited degree.

If we consider the medical profession, we can see how readily the concept of karma-yoga can be applied. Naturally, those who work in such caring roles should be adequately rewarded for their service in order to ensure their well-being and that of their family. The primary motivation, however, should be to serve those under their care, and here we can see how any form of caring profession fits Krishna's prescription for karma-yoga. Motives will generally be mixed, but at their best such professionals will put the welfare of others before their own interests.

In other professions the application of karma-yoga can be a little less obvious. However, in most walks of life the idea of work as duty in the service of others can be applied. Society depends for its welfare on the positive participation of each individual. Moreover, those in positions of authority can affect those subordinate to them by the attitude they display towards them. Kind words, encouragement, and good humour, along with a willingness to assist in times of need, all serve to bring happiness and contentment to colleagues, and should encourage others to conduct themselves in a similar manner. Business people can take inspiration from the concept of karma-yoga. Their business can bring a good livelihood along with a responsibility to employees who they serve by providing employment and security.

It might appear that the dharmic emphasis on compassion and non-harming is not appropriate for those in the military or security services where violent means are sometimes essential. Again though, we can draw on the Gita's idea of karma-yoga in order to understand how such professions are compatible with the pursuit of dharma. The Mahabharata, and the Bhagavad-gita in particular, shows us how the military profession can be undertaken in a manner that is in accordance with the values of compassion and non-harming. On the battlefield at Kurukshetra, Arjuna wages war against Duryodhana, a king who shows scant respect for the values of dharma, a man who interprets dharma as naked self-interest.

Both of these warriors undertake a similar course of action in seeking victory over the other, and yet the conclusion of the text is that Arjuna is a practitioner of karma-yoga, and a man of dharma, whilst Duryodhana is represented as his antithesis, a man who forsakes dharma in pursuit of personal gain.

The difference is motivation rather than action. Arjuna fights to protect the innocent from the aggression of wrongdoers; he fights out of compassion for the weak, and so that they do not suffer any further harm; he fights in a mood of detachment, without selfish desire, because he adheres to the edicts of karma-yoga. In the same way, those who serve in the military can regard their actions as a service to society, protecting the weak from the aggressive and belligerent. At times it is necessary for trained men and women to use violent means as the only way in which protection can be afforded.

The vital point is that action of this type must be undertaken only out of a sense of duty and service to others, to preserve the well-being of others. In this way we can observe how Hindu ethics provide guidance for those who serve in the military and related professions. Again this is not a set of rules and regulations but of principles on which such rules will be established for each set of circumstances. Once again, the demand is for intelligence and integrity in order to properly establish the correct course of action that is pursuant of the ideal of dharma. Violence is in many ways the antithesis of dharma, but at the same time absolute pacifism seems an implausible doctrine to apply to the world as we find it. The challenge is to establish when the use of violent means is genuinely in accordance with dharma, and to understand how those in the military may come to engage in acts of violence whilst sustaining their sense of integrity and service to humanity as a whole.

Exercises

1. How relevant are Hindu ethics in the modern professional setting?

2. How might the chaplain respond to the criticism that Hinduism is a religion without any fixed rules?

GUILT, TRAGEDY, AND MORAL IMPROVEMENT

There is a strong argument to suggest that the pervasive religious emphasis on guilt is derived primarily from Christian theology, with its notions of original sin and redemption through the death of Christ. In traditional Christian thought, all human beings are deemed to be sinful because of the original sin of Adam, and it is this sin that was the direct cause of the appearance and suffering of Jesus Christ. Moreover, for the unredeemed this inherent sin leads to absolute and eternal damnation in the fires of hell. Many, perhaps a majority, of Christians today no longer hold absolutely to this traditional teaching, but there seems little doubt that it has left a legacy of religious guilt, and a heavy consciousness of sin and imperfection. Many will no doubt feel that this sense of guilt is a positive force, and that in today's secular society a greater sense of guilt over our actions, and lack of action, would be a positive force. The danger is that when the sense of guilt becomes too pressing it can destroy our sense of delight in the good things of the world and lead us to equate all pleasure with sin.

From the Hindu perspective, the concept of guilt is rather different, and one should avoid being drawn into relying on simplistic equations between Christian and Hindu thought. Traditional Hindu teachings suggest that there are four broad goals to be achieved in human life, *kama*, *artha*, dharma, and *moksha*; fulfilment of material desire, the accumulation of wealth, righteous living, and the spiritual pursuit of liberation from rebirth. Some authorities add *bhakti*, devotion to God, as a fifth goal of life, but in most cases this is assumed to fall under the fourth heading of *moksha*.

From the Hindu point of view there is no direct opposition between pleasure and spirituality, and enjoying the pleasures of life is not regarded as inherently sinful, provided one's actions do not violate the precepts of dharma. Rather, what is sought is a state of balance between the four goals of life, although it is accepted that dharma and *moksha* stand above the other two, and, where possible, should be given precedence. An interesting point is made by Vatsyayana in his introduction to the Kama Sutras. He praises *kama*, the fulfilment of desire, as something all human beings should aspire to, but he also warns that when that pursuit becomes obsessive and overwhelming, it can bring harm and destruction. He cites the example of Ravana from the Ramayana. Ravana was intelligent, learned, artistic, and a devoted performer of religious ritual. However, he became so obsessed with the pursuit of pleasure that he lost any sense of balance that he might once have had, and became wholly indifferent to any idea of dharma. As a result, a successful life became one of folly and wrongdoing, which led eventually to his own destruction.

We need to consider the Hindu belief in rebirth, which allows much greater scope for gradual development. Most Hindus do not expect to achieve spiritual perfection in this lifetime, but hope instead to improve their moral and spiritual standing in order to achieve favourable rebirth, and further progress in the next life. The result is that moral perfection is never expected, and this tends to detract from any sense of guilt. There may be regret over failures to adhere to the highest standards of dharma, and any shame caused to the family thereby, but it is accepted that there is always scope for improvement, and this upward progression, moral and spiritual, is the real aim of life.

One chaplain gives the following instructive example:

> A Jain monk agreed to give a talk to a group of students I was conducting on an educational trip to India. At the end of the presentation, I offered the speaker a small donation on behalf of the college, but he replied that as a naked mendicant, he had no use for money or possessions. He then suggested

> that each of the students should make a small pledge to improve his or her own life. I was a little apprehensive about this, but what he requested was that each of them should promise to be vegetarian for one day, or perhaps even one day a week, or else give up alcohol for one day.

The point here is that he did not ask for absolute abstention from meat or alcohol. There was no sense of deep sin, but rather the request for some gradual movement in the direction of dharma, and this, in many ways, typifies the Hindu approach to morality and guilt.

Some might feel uncomfortable over this approach, regarding it as too lax, but on the other hand we might suggest that guilt is not a particularly positive sentiment in the search for progress. From the Hindu perspective, moral improvement is always possible, and this can be most easily achieved in small stages rather than by a sudden conversion to the path of righteousness. Rather than feeling an overpowering sense of guilt, one can instead accept one's own shortcomings, and do as much as possible to improve by moving closer to the ideal standard of dharma. Moreover, however great a philanthropist one may be, there is always scope to do a little more, to help a few more people.

Tragedy, particularly where it involves the loss of a loved one, can also cause feelings of guilt. We may feel that we did not do enough for them, or spend enough time with them while they were alive, and now the opportunity to address this shortcoming is gone. This is natural, but in most cases there is no real need for self-reproach. We could all do more on behalf of our family, but this is often difficult, and again excessive feelings of guilt are rarely helpful or productive. Again, the main point is to try to move some way in the right direction in the future.

Hindu teachings consistently remind us that tragedy and grief are an inevitable part of human life and, as far as possible, one must try to develop a mood of stoicism by understanding the higher existence. Faith in God, and a belief in an afterlife, can comfort those who have experienced tragedy, but at the same time it can be insensitive to over-emphasise philosophical ideas at a time of heightened emotion. Sometimes simple comfort is the best one can offer. This approach reflects the idea of dharma as compassion, kindness, and concern for the well-being of others.

This can then be combined with a more philosophical approach, when questions of this type arise in response to personal tragedy, or when they appear to be most appropriate. According to the Bhagavad-gita:

matra-sparshas tu kaunteya
sitoshna-sukha-duhkha-dah
agamapayino 'nityas
tams titikshasva bharata

> It is contact with the senses, Kaunteya, which leads to sensations of heat and cold, and pleasure and pain. Being impermanent, these sensations appear and then disappear, and one must learn to endure them, Bharata. (Bhagavad-gita 2.14)

The message here is stoicism; in life we experience joy and tragedy, and the aim should be to transcend suffering and elation by developing a mood of detachment from the world. This idea is frequently encountered in Hindu texts, but it may well be that consideration of the eternal nature of the soul, and of the mercy of God, will be more effective in providing consolation. Here is another quotation from the Bhagavad-gita:

dehino 'smin yatha dehe
kaumaram yauvanam jara
tatha dehantara-praptir
dhiras tatra na muhyati

> For the embodied soul, present in this body, there is childhood, youth, and then old age, and in the same way [after death] it then acquires a different body. One who is wise is not confused about this. (Bhagavad-gita 2.13)

In this verse, Krishna comforts Arjuna by emphasising the eternal nature of the living being. All of us must suffer the tragedies of death and bereavement, but the sense of loss may be mitigated by understanding that the individual who passed away has moved on to another life, or may even have been elevated to existence as an associate of the supreme Lord.

Most Hindus tend to be devotionally inclined, with their worship focused on Krishna, Shiva, Rama, or Parvati, and comfort in the face of tragedy can be gained by the consciousness of a merciful deity who oversees everything that happens in this world. Death is inevitable, and so is the loss of loved ones, but for those who have faith in the mercy and kindness of an all-powerful God there can be a sense that all will be well under the protection of the Lord. Again such words of comfort are to be found in the Bhagavad-gita:

sarva-dharman parityajya
mam ekam sharanam vraja
aham tva sarva-papebhyo
mokshayishyami ma shuchah

> Giving up all other forms of religion, you can find shelter with Me alone. I will deliver you from all the evils of the world. Do not be afraid. (Bhagavad-gita 18.66)

Such words of comfort can help relieve the suffering that must follow life's inevitable tragedies, and the notion of a loving God can be particularly important at such times of grief. Here the phrase *ma shuchah*, meaning 'do not fear', or 'do not worry', is particularly significant as it reveals that Krishna, as the loving God, is always watching over his devotees, and is concerned to ensure their absolute well-being.

As mentioned previously, the Hindu tradition provides complex rites and rituals for funerals, and for providing for the well-being of departed loved ones in their future existence; these latter are known as the *shraddha* offerings. It would be highly advisable for Hindu chaplains to make a study of these rites, to become familiar with the passages of sacred text that are recited, and thereby be able to explain to family members the significance of each phase of the ritual. Tragedy is as much a part of human life as the joys it brings, and an important part of the chaplain's vocation is to understand and to employ the resources provided by the Hindu tradition that can help in the amelioration of the suffering that follows tragic events.

To return to our discussion of morality, guilt, and moral improvement, we should note the Hindu view that worldly conduct, and the values we live by, are not a purely material concern. Moral improvement can be enforced to some extent by the rigid implementation of rules at a social level, but in reality it is a matter of personal transformation, and this is primarily a spiritual process. From the Hindu perspective, the aim is to become inherently righteous rather than someone who is forced to act in a virtuous manner due to social or economic pressures. Those who are iniquitous by nature will damage others and speak vicious words, whilst the righteous person is instinctively drawn to virtue. If we change ourselves, then the transformation of our moral standards follow.

Throughout Hindu texts, it is asserted that living in accordance with the precepts of dharma is both the means of attaining spiritual awakening, as well as being a consequence of that enlightenment. In the famous discussion that takes place at the start of the Katha Upanishad, Mrityu informs Nachiketas that he is qualified to absorb the highest level of realised knowledge, the knowledge of the soul, because he is free from the corrupting influence of selfish tendencies. In other words, those who tend toward iniquity are not able to transcend the world or attain the highest levels of spiritual awakening. Similarly, the famous South Indian text, Shiva-Jñana-Bodham, states when a person performs righteous acts, Shiva, existing in the hearts of all, will awaken the liberating knowledge within that person. We find the same point being reasserted within the text of the Mahabharata:

yada na kurute bhavam
yada chasman na bibhyeti
karmana manasa vacha
brahma sampadyate tada

> When he is never the cause of any harmful condition for any living being with his actions, thoughts, or words, then he has attained Brahman. (Mahabharata 12.254.17)

This verse reveals the intimate connection that exists between living in accordance with the precepts of dharma and attaining spiritual realisation, referred to here by the word Brahman. This way of living may be the means by which Brahman is attained, or it may be symptomatic of that realisation, but in either case we can see how moral improvement and spiritual awakening are regarded as two parts of the same process.

grihastho brahmachari va
vanaprastho 'tha va punah
ya icchen moksham asthastum
uttamam vrittim ashrayet

abhayam sarva-bhutebhyo
dattva naishkarmyam acharet
sarva-bhuta-hito maitrah
sarvendriya-yato munih

> Whether he be a householder, unmarried student, or retired to the forest, anyone who wishes to achieve liberation from rebirth must adhere to the most perfect way of life.
>
> Only when he bestows the gift of fearlessness on all living beings can the sage achieve freedom from karma. He should act for the welfare of all beings, show kindness to all, and bring his senses under control (Mahabharata 14.46.17–18)

Here again we see how the dharmic virtues are represented as being an essential element in the process of acquiring spiritual enlightenment. The explanation for this is given in the Bhagavad-gita, which offers an insight into why people are drawn into acts of wickedness, even if striving for the highest goals of life.

arjuna uvacha
atha kena prayukto 'yam
papam charati purushah
anicchan api varshneya
balad iva niyojitah

sri bhagavan uvacha
kama esha krodha esha
rajoguna-samudbhavah
mahashano maha-papma
viddhy enam iha vairinam

> Arjuna said: 'What is it that impels a person so that he acts sinfully, even though he has no desire to do so, Varshneya [Krishna], compelling him to act in that way as if by force?'
>
> The Lord said: 'It is desire, it is anger; this arises from the *guna* known as *rajas* (the quality of passion).

> You should know this as a mighty devouring force, a great source of sin; it is the enemy of the world.' (Bhagavad-gita 3.36–7)

The idea here is that moral turpitude arises from the intensity of our desires for the pleasures of life. As has been stated earlier, there is nothing inherently wicked about enjoying pleasure, but here we learn that where the desire for such pleasure becomes too strong, then moral conduct will inevitably be inhibited. Here again we might note the example of Ravana, as depicted in the Ramayana, a person who was so overwhelmed with the fulfilment of base desires that he lost all concern for dharma. Most people desire to be righteous, but, as we learn here, the strength of the desires that oppress us make it very difficult to achieve that goal. The solution then must be to somehow withdraw ourselves, at least to some extent, from our usual absorption with material gain, reputation, and the fulfilment of desires. How can this be achieved? The Bhagavad-gita offers a solution:

vishaya vinivartante
niraharasya dehinah
rasa-varjam raso 'py asya
param drishtva nivartate

> The objects of pleasure do not touch the embodied soul who abstains from them. In this way one can restrict one's inclination, although the inclination will remain. But after perceiving the Supreme, one completely renounces such desires. (Bhagavad-gita 2.59)

The suggestion here is that if one gains some experience of the higher, spiritual reality postulated by Hindu teachings, then one's inclinations toward the pleasures of the world will begin to subside. And when such inclinations diminish, then there is real hope of moral improvement.

Of course, one must not presume that this is the only solution to the question of moral improvement offered by the Hindu tradition. There are many passages and teachings that focus solely on the issue of dharma, and living one's life in accordance with the precepts of dharma, simply because it is the right and proper thing to do, without any reference to God, spirituality, enlightenment, or liberation from rebirth. Nonetheless, it is interesting, and important, to note that from the Hindu perspective there can be no sense of true spiritual awakening unless it is accompanied by a transformation in morality and dedication to good work.

Exercises

1. What approaches can the chaplain adopt when supporting persons afflicted by tragedy in their lives?
2. What resources can the Hindu chaplain draw upon in confronting situations of grief and tragedy?

MORAL PURITY AND IMPURITY

The question of determinism looms large in relation to Indian religion, primarily because of the doctrines of karma and rebirth, and what they imply about human psychology. Essentially, the problem is this: The doctrine of karma teaches that one's present embodiment and psychology are a direct result of actions, including words and thoughts, performed in a previous existence. Different views are expressed in different texts as to exactly how this takes place. In theistic Hinduism, the idea seems to be that karma is very much under the control of the supreme deity, and that he has the power to change the destiny of each individual. We find this view expressed in the later verses of the Bhagavad-gita's sixteenth chapter. From this perspective, karma is understood as a form of divine justice dealt out to the sinners and the righteous alike. Teachings of a more philosophical nature, particularly those related to the yoga system, give a rather different view, arguing that every action performed is preceded by a particular state of consciousness, such as compassion preceding an act of charity, or hatred preceding an act of violence. This state of consciousness then subtly reshapes the individual identity, so that action performed shapes the nature of future existence. In effect, one is recreating oneself moment by moment as each new state of consciousness leaves its own subtle impression.

In relation to moral purity, this means that there is a strong argument to suggest that from a Hindu perspective one's individual nature is predetermined, and cannot be changed. One may be given fine words of instruction, but cannot transform one's own inherent nature, which is predestined at the time of birth. In this regard, it is interesting to note the words used in the opening verses of sixteenth chapter of the Gita:

tejah kshama dhritih shaucham
adroho nati-manita
bhavanti sampadam daivim
ajatasya bharata

dambho darpo 'bhimanas cha
krodhah parushyam eva cha
ajñanam chabhijatasya
partha sampadam asurim

daivi sampad vimokshaya
nibandhayasuri mata
ma shuchah sampadam daivim
abhijato 'si pandava

Energy, patience, resolve, purity, the absence of malice and of arrogance; these constitute the godly disposition of one who is born with this nature, Bharata.

Deceit, arrogance, pride, anger, harshness, and ignorance, Partha, are the *asuric* disposition of one who is born with that nature, O Pandava.

> The godly disposition leads to liberation, but the *asuric* disposition is regarded as a cause of bondage. Do not be concerned about this, Pandava, for you have been born with the godly disposition. (Bhagavad-gita 16.3–5)

We have already looked at this passage in our consideration of moral perspectives, but at this stage in the discussion, the point I would particularly draw attention to is the use of the word *abhijatah* in all three of the verses cited. *Abhijata* is a compound derived from the Sanskrit verb *'ja'*, which means 'to take birth', and hence the conclusion here would be that one's inner disposition, and one's state of moral purity, are determined from the moment of birth. Hindu religious philosophy considers there to be three *gunas*, or inherent qualities, in all things material, named as *sattva*, *rajas*, and *tamas* (purity, passion, and darkness). The combination of these three qualities in each person determines his or her *sva-bhava* (inherent nature) and again it is stated that this combination, tending toward purity, passion, or darkness, is predetermined at the time of birth. As an interesting aside, we might note that this is the point of view expressed by the prophet Jeremiah in the Old Testament of the Bible, 'Can the Ethiopian change his skin, or the leopard his spots? Then may ye also do good, that are accustomed to do evil.' (Jeremiah, 13.23)

From this brief analysis, one might conclude that Hindu thought is deeply deterministic, and, concomitantly, that moral purity and impurity are predetermined at birth. This, however, is not the whole picture, and in the Mahabharata we find a slightly different perspective being presented. The question of destiny and free will is one that figures prominently in the Mahabharata, notably Dhritarashtra's tendency to attribute his shortcomings to the predetermined force of destiny. In the thirteenth book, however, the subject is addressed directly in the form of a treatise on whether or not it is possible for a person's desires and actions to directly affect any outcome.

In Chapter 6 of Book 13, Yudhishthira asks Bhishma about the relative significance of destiny and free will in human life, and in reply Bhishma refers to an ancient account of a discussion between Vasishtha and Brahma on that very subject. In that conversation, destiny is compared to a ploughed field and endeavour to the sowing of seed in that field. The field of destiny may be perfectly ploughed, and hence quite fertile, but unless the work of sowing the seed is undertaken there will be no positive result. Likewise, the field may not be particularly fertile, but by hard work and endeavour a crop may still be grown. The point of the metaphor used is to show that although destiny is a powerful force in our lives it is not absolutely binding on the individual.

The Mahabharata presents differing degrees of emphasis on the strength of the influence of destiny over human life, but the conclusion would seem to be that although the qualities we are born with do have a significant effect on our character and fortune, the endeavour to improve both will still yield profitable results. When we apply this understanding to the issue of moral purity and impurity, we can observe that different persons are born with differing dispositions, but for each individual the possibility of a move toward greater purity is possible, and is to be encouraged at all times. The debate over birth or experience, nature or nurture, is one that is still very much current in the modern world, and there are few today who believe that an individual's personality is formed entirely by upbringing and experience. We can certainly assert that this is the Hindu perspective as well, as karma and the *gunas* one is born with exert a powerful effect throughout one's life, but at the same time life experience and personal endeavour can have an equally significant influence.

Hence when moral impurity is encountered, we can be certain that every person has the potential for change and improvement. Moral impurity may be the result of the inherent nature a person is born with, but positive and negative experiences in life will also have a profound influence. As the poet W.H. Auden states, 'Those to whom evil is done, do evil in return.' We might also refer to a quotation from the Bhagavad-gita that we looked at previously, which gives some explanation as to why a person might breach the principles of dharma. When Krishna is asked why it is that a person will develop a tendency to act in an iniquitous manner, he replies (3.37) that it is desire and anger together that produce that tendency. Hence we might argue that it is the intense desire for material gain, and for fame and reputation, that are the root cause of moral impurity, and again, if we turn to the Ramayana, we can notice the character of Ravana as one obsessed by desire and therefore almost devoid of any sense of moral purity. If a person can be somehow guided away from the intensity of material desires, then there is hope of resolving the issue of moral impurity, at least to some degree.

In considering how moral impurity can be confronted, we must first make the point that each individual is different, and may respond differently to differing forms of stimulus toward moral improvement. Therefore the chaplain's first task is to listen carefully to a person's concerns, and perhaps explanations for the courses of action adopted. The chaplain is not a guru or religious leader, and as such has no inherent authority to dictate how any person should live his or her life. All he can do is to listen and to advise, and in doing this he needs to think carefully about the best approach. A direct didactic approach, laying down the rules that have been broken and must be adhered to, will rarely, if ever, be effective, and this is not really in line with the Hindu idea of ethical conduct, which is relative rather than absolute. Even in the Bhagavad-gita, where the counsellor is Krishna, the supreme deity, the words '*iti me matih*', meaning 'that is my opinion', are frequently encountered. So even God does not deal in absolute statements or demands, but rather offers valuable advice and productive material for personal contemplation.

The chaplain must therefore firstly listen and try to comprehend the reasons why a person, who will generally still claim some adherence to a Hindu identity, appears to be deviating quite markedly from the standards set by the precepts of dharma. It may be that it is simply a matter of lacking knowledge of what those precepts are, or of how their own personal conduct represents a breach of those standards. More usually, however, it will require a careful and measured discussion of conduct in general, so that the individual does not feel personally vilified, and a broad consideration of how the precepts of dharma can best be implemented in the contemporary world. The hope must be that discussions of this type will encourage the other party to think carefully about morality, and his or her own way of life and personal conduct. This will be particularly useful in encounters with young Hindus, who are often idealistic, but unclear as to how these ideals should be translated into appropriate lifestyle choices.

Another approach may be to refer to sources of authority such as sacred text, family elders, gurus, and religious leaders. This should only be done, however, after some initial discussion has taken place, so that the chaplain can gauge which of these will be likely to provide a positive response. Some Hindus regard the ancient texts as inappropriate for today's world, some are mistrustful of gurus and institutional leaders, and some see the family elders as not having a proper grasp of the nature and requirements of the modern world. Sacred text can, in many circumstances, be a particularly useful source to employ in such discussions, and the chaplain would be well advised to build up a stock of passages and narratives that can be drawn into discussions of this type. There need not even be a strong didactic element to these discussions, unless it seems particularly appropriate, and individuals can be left to draw their own conclusions – though perhaps with a little subtle prompting.

The main point to be derived from this consideration of Hindu approaches to moral impurity is that there are few, if any, people who are wholly beyond redemption, and this will apply particularly to those the Hindu chaplain will come into contact with. The Ramayana does offer us the example of Ravana, who was given extensive instruction in dharma by his brother Vibhishana but only became enraged by this good advice. Fortunately, however, we will encounter relatively few Ravanas or Duryodhanas, and it is to be hoped that every individual one comes into contact with can be helped, albeit only in some small way, to move toward the standards of dharma we have discussed in this section of the course.

Exercise

1. According to Hindu teachings, what are the main causes of moral impurity?
2. How should the Hindu chaplain confront moral impurity? What the resources available to assist in this challenge?

5. APPLIED HINDU PSYCHOLOGY

✻

Here we turn our attention to Hindu ideas on psychology and consider how such ideas may be used by chaplains in their work in the community. We begin by looking at traditional Hindu views on the human psyche, drawing primarily on the teachings of the *samkhya* systems and then briefly consider yoga practice and the ways in which this can be used to bring about tranquillity. This leads into further consideration of the chaplain's work in relation to coping strategies during times of stress, spiritual stagnation, learning, and growth. We end with a look at the two great Hindu epics, the Ramayana and Mahabharata, and discuss how these texts can form a part of discussions based around the idea of spiritual progression.

HINDU VIEWS ON PSYCHOLOGICAL COACHING

Hindu ideas on psychology are for the most part derived from the teachings of the *samkhya* and yoga systems, the earliest of which are to be found in the later books of the Mahabharata. In *samkhya* philosophy, and in many of the early Sanskrit texts, the human psyche is divided into a number of differing faculties, each of which has a particular function. Firstly, there are the five senses through which knowledge of the external world is acquired moment by moment. These are listed as sight, hearing, smell, touch, and taste. The sensations experienced by these senses are immediately transmitted to what we might refer to as the mind, the *manas* in Sanskrit. On the basis of past experience, the *manas* is able to identify each of the sensations as it arrives via the senses, and thereby provide an awareness of the present situation. The *manas*, however, does not reflect on or make decisions on the basis of the sensations it identifies, for there is a further mental faculty, the *buddhi*, which performs this function. The term *buddhi* is usually translated as intelligence, intellect, or understanding, but we might also consider it to be the individual personality of a human being. *Samkhya* treatises assert that the *buddhi* is as close to the true self, the *atman* or *purusha*, as anything that occurs in the overall mental faculty, but nonetheless it is still material, and hence still shaped and affected by the world around us. Each experience we undergo leaves a subtle impression on the *buddhi*, and, moreover, the *buddhi* transmigrates to another body at the time of death, as a subtle covering of the *atman*, thereby carrying these impressions with it into another life.

The *buddhi* receives information, derived from sensory perceptions, from the *manas*, and makes decisions as to the action to be taken. It thinks and it learns, it is in effect the person I know myself to be with all my own characteristic traits. This personality is close to the soul, but it is still affected by experiences and perceptions, and by the disposition of the three *gunas* with which it is born. It is for this reason that each person is born with a personality that is partially formed, although of course this will undergo marked transformation as a result of life experiences. The true self, the *atman* or *purusha*, is entirely transcendental; it is changeless and aloof, and is identical in each individual person. The aim of the spiritual quest of the *samkhya* and yoga systems is to gain a direct awareness of the existence of the *atman*, and thereby transcend the fluctuating forms that characterise existence in this world.

When we come to consider psychological coaching, then this understanding of the Hindu perspective on the psyche may not be directly of use, but it is still worth keeping in mind when we consider the wider subject of human nature;

there is also the possibility that it may arise as a subject for deeper conversations. Within the broad Hindu traditions, we find that psychological help being given for those in difficulty or in distress usually takes the form of the presentation and emphasis of philosophical ideas. There are many examples of lamenting individuals being helped by wise persons who reveal higher truths about our existence. Perhaps the best known example of this is to be found in Krishna's counselling of Arjuna in the Bhagavad-gita; the Mahabharata also contains many similar examples.

The Gita opens with Arjuna lamenting over the position he finds himself in, being forced to choose between giving up his royal position and waging war against those who are his friends and relatives. Krishna's response is firstly philosophical, reminding Arjuna of the existence of the soul as a deathless entity, and of the doctrine of transmigration. From this starting point, he quickly moves on to urge Arjuna to adopt a more detached view of the world, understanding its temporary nature, the ideal of duty, and the omnipresence of a loving deity. The Bhagavad-gita has been referred to as a perfect example of mature counselling, as it shows how an individual can be gradually drawn toward a more detached view of the world and his own position in it. The present problems may seem to be unbearable but by detached reflection, one can come to place them within a wider context, and to realise that they are not insurmountable. The Hindu tradition is particularly well equipped to provide a basis for reflection of this type, as its teachings, be they on dharma, the nature of the self, or on the love of God, can all be highly effective in invoking a more circumspect view of the immediate situation.

This approach is sometimes referred to as developing a mood of mindfulness, a modern technique that is rooted in Indian religion. From the Hindu perspective, mindfulness means developing an awareness of oneself, of one's true situation in life, and of the passions that shape our motives in acting and speaking as we do. It is very easy to develop this perception in relation to other people, but the technique here is to see oneself in true perspective, with as little bias and prejudice as possible. This may be achieved through the acquisition of philosophical and religious insights, such as those presented in the Bhagavad-gita and Upanishads, or it may be that the techniques of yoga meditation will help in this respect.

Today, most yoga teaching focuses on the physical side of the tradition. This is often referred to as postural yoga, but in the ancient teachings of Patañjali, as found in his Yoga Sutra, the emphasis is very much on the mind and on mindfulness. The Yoga Sutra is an immensely complex text that has spiritual transcendence as its primary aim, but nonetheless some simple techniques of mindfulness can be extrapolated from its four chapters. Essentially, Patañjali's aim is to show how one can gain mastery over the wandering mind, so that it can be fixed exactly where one wishes it to remain. We find a similar idea expressed more simply within the sixth chapter of the Bhagavad-gita. Of course, gaining this type of mastery over the mind is not a simple endeavour and one will surely find that it is achieved only very gradually. The point is that the endeavour alone can be of psychological value, even if the success achieved by it is only very limited.

Hindu chaplains do not need to develop any significant expertise in yoga practices in order to offer them as a possible aid to those they encounter. The only requirement on sitting posture that Patañjali demands is that it be firm and comfortable, so that the practitioner can engage in the process of meditation. This can be done by using a simple mantra that is familiar to the practitioner, perhaps, *om namah shivaya,* or, *om namo bhagavate vasudevaya*. The main point is not the mantra itself, but the process of concentration, so that one endeavours to keep the mind fixed without deviation on each of the syllables as the mantra is run through the mind. Constant levels of concentration are very difficult to achieve, but gradual practice can lead to greater mental control and a sense of mental relaxation that is highly therapeutic. An associated technique is to focus on particular qualities or facets of one's character in order to gain greater insight into how one leads life and the things that should be valued. At this point we would advise a careful study of Chapter 6 of the Bhagavad-gita in order to acquire a more rounded understanding of the techniques employed in the classical yoga tradition.

There are different forms of psychological counselling the chaplain will learn to employ, and hopefully experience will add to the level of expertise. From the Hindu perspective, however, one should probably emphasise philosophical counselling about the true nature of the world, and the developing of a mood of detachment and transcendence. Some basic knowledge of yoga techniques and yoga philosophy will also be valuable, and again we would emphasise the importance of a thorough study of Hindu belief and practice in order to expand the range of resources the chaplain will be able to draw upon.

Exercise

1. How valuable is knowledge of Hindu ideas on the human mind and spirit for the chaplain's task of psychological coaching?

COPING STRATEGIES, SPIRITUAL STAGNATION, LEARNING, AND GROWTH

Life can be beset with difficulties that cause us stress, anxiety, and doubts about how we should live. One role played by religion is providing coping strategies at times of difficulty, and one of the most important roles of the chaplain is to assist individuals in making effective use of such strategies. At the most basic level, the chaplain must make use of the dharmic quality of compassion, showing sympathy and listening carefully to those who wish to talk about their troubles. This, along with a sympathetic response, can often help enormously in allowing individuals to cope and to see that there is hope for future.

Beyond this essential prerequisite, the chaplain may also refer to specifically Hindu teachings about the nature of beyond the day-to-day situations we encounter. This must be done with care in order to avoid any suggestion that the present troubles are insignificant and not worthy of sympathy. At an appropriate point in the conversation, however, it may be possible to carry the discussion forward and introduce philosophical insights concerning the higher truths of human existence. Ideally, such conversations should be introduced by the distressed person so that the chaplain responds and guides rather than dictating the line of discussion.

Themes that can be pursued include an emphasis on dharma as the highest aim in life, the transcendent nature of the soul, and the compassion shown by a loving God. Our earlier considerations of the precepts of Sanatana Dharma have revealed an emphasis on acting and speaking in a way that brings support to others, and goes some little way toward relieving the sufferings of the world. References to the importance of dharma will not always be appropriate for persons in distress, but it can be helpful to consider these higher goals, which can help in transcending present difficulties while remaining firmly rooted in this world.

Another coping strategy comes in the form of considering the higher, spiritual nature of our existence. This is particularly useful for persons attempting to cope with bereavement or illness. It is this approach that Krishna employs in the opening verses of his discussion with Arjuna in the Bhagavad-gita, although the tone he initially adopts reflects the closeness of their relationship, and will not be appropriate in most cases. These verses are from Chapter 2 of the Bhagavad-gita.

> 11. The Lord said: Grieving for that which should not be lamented over, you speak words that appear to be wise. But learned men grieve for neither the living nor the dead.

12. There was never a time when I did not exist, nor you, nor these lords of men; nor shall any of us cease to exist in the future.

13. For the embodied soul present in this body, there is childhood, youth, and then old age, and in the same way acquires a different body [at death]. One who is wise is not confused about this.

14. It is contact with the senses, Kaunteya, which leads to sensations of heat and cold, and pleasure and pain. Being impermanent, these sensations appear and then disappear, and you must learn to endure them, Bharata.

15. If these sensations do not distract a person, O best of men, and he can remain equal in sorrow and happiness, then such a wise person gains the state of immortality.

16. That which is unreal never comes into being, and that which is real never ceases to be. Those who perceive the truth can recognise this conclusion concerning these two.

17. You must understand this indestructible principle that pervades the whole world. No one can bring about the destruction of this unchanging principle.

18. This embodied soul is eternal, indestructible, and unlimited. The bodies it inhabits, however, must come to an end. Therefore fight, O Bharata.

19. Neither the person who thinks that this is the killer, nor the one who thinks it is killed, properly understands it, for it does not kill, and it cannot be killed.

20. It is never born and it never dies. It is existing now and it will never cease to exist. It is unborn, eternal, everlasting, and most ancient. It is not killed when the body is killed.

21. How can a person who properly understands it as indestructible and eternal cause the death of anyone or kill anyone? What will he cause the death of? What will he kill?

22. Just as a man casts aside old clothes and puts on others that are new, so the embodied soul casts aside old bodies and accepts other new ones.

23. Weapons cannot cut it, fire cannot burn it, water cannot make it wet, and wind cannot dry it.

24. This cannot be cut, it cannot be burned, and it cannot be moistened or dried. It is eternal, all-pervasive, fixed, immovable, and everlasting.

25. It is said that it is imperceptible and inconceivable, and it is not subject to transformation. Understanding it in this way, you should lament no more.

26. And even if you think that it is born repeatedly, and repeatedly dies, still you should not lament over it, O mighty one.

27. For one who has been born, death is certain, and for one who has died, birth is certain. Therefore you should not lament over something that cannot be avoided.

28. In the beginning, living beings are not manifest. They become manifest in the interim stage, Bharata,

> but at their end, they become non-manifest again. Why should there be lamentation over this?
>
> 29. By some wonder a person may perceive it, by some wonder another person may speak of it, and by some wonder yet another person may come to hear about it. But another person may not understand it, even after hearing about it.
>
> 30. It is impossible to kill this embodied soul that is always present within the bodies of all beings. Therefore you should not lament over any living being.

These verses relate primarily to the immortality of the soul, and they are presented here as an illustration of the type of passage that can be referred to so that a person may come to develop an effective coping strategy. The tone of the passage may appear a little harsh for some people, and it will often be a good idea to either summarise contents or else to direct people to relevant sections of the text so that they develop their own responses to the teachings encountered.

As has been mentioned before, most Hindus are devotionally inclined, having faith in the love of God and the protection the deity will give to those who worship and revere him. At times of severe distress, this faith may be difficult or even impossible to sustain. Such situations require the chaplain to use skill and sensitivity in order to provide reassurance, for a loss of faith will only add to the feelings of distress. Again it is better to avoid didactic lectures, and instead gently guide such a person toward some understanding of the nature of God and the role played by the deity. Once again, a detailed knowledge of major texts will prove invaluable to the chaplain in providing this necessary guidance.

In discussing coping strategies, our main aim has been to show the need for compassion to be kept to the fore at all times, and then to show how religious teachings can provide an effective basis for dealing with life's crises. The point is that it is often useful to try to take a step back from the emotional impact of our situation, and to view our position from a slightly more detached and philosophical perspective. Guidance in this endeavour must be given with great sensitivity and intelligence, but the realisations referred to in Hindu teachings can be of immense value in providing comfort and helping to relieve the stress and anxiety that we all face at some time.

Spiritual stagnation is something that will almost certainly afflict every religious-minded person at some stage of life, for it is almost impossible to sustain a high level of enthusiasm at all times. It is a widely observed phenomenon that religious enthusiasm in a younger person can tend to evaporate with the onset of middle age and the numerous cares associated with career and family life. Some may have bad experiences of religious groups or individuals, and decide to have nothing more to do with spirituality and religious life. The chaplain may encounter many who will express doubts and misgivings about the value of religion and express the view that it is of little value for the life they lead.

When encountering individuals in this position, chaplains need to employ their powers of sympathy and intelligence, and be able to draw on a wide ranging knowledge of the Hindu religious tradition. For example, a person may state that he has no interest in spirituality because he no longer believes in God. In such a situation, the chaplain might turn the discussion toward the idea of dharma, and seek to show that the Hindu tradition is not just about a supreme deity but is a multi-faceted ideology from which almost anyone can draw inspiration. If a person finds it difficult to believe in the stories or anthropomorphic forms of God he or she was brought up with, then there are other forms of theology to refer to, perhaps most notably Shankaracharya's teachings on the omnipresent nature of the supreme Brahman. The fact that Hindu spirituality appears in many different guises allows the chaplain to guide virtually any person encountered toward some form of spiritual awakening or revival. The challenge is to broaden one's knowledge of the resources the tradition makes available to us, and then to be able to judge the type of ideas that will inspire each individual to break free from spiritual stagnation, be it Vedanta, dharma, love of God, yoga techniques, or the manifold and varied philosophical teachings available to us.

The potential for learning is always with us, either through study and reflection, through listening to advice and guidance, through yoga practice, or simply by gaining experience in life. Another task the chaplain can perform is helping others to gain that learning, both by giving guidance and by advising individuals about the resources available to them, particularly those from sacred texts. In the latter case, the emphasis is probably best placed on the Upanishads, Bhagavad-gita, Mahabharata, and Ramayana.

Where the chaplain is working with student groups or Hindu youth groups, then opportunities should be taken to enhance learning and understanding of the tradition. If there is sufficient enthusiasm, study groups can be set up to explore Hindu religious teachings and the ideas presented in different textual sources. Discussion groups are useful as these can provide opportunities for young people to express their own misgivings and to seek responses to questions and criticisms from outsiders they may have been confronted with. It is often the case that young Hindus are presented with difficult questions and one of the roles of the chaplain is to provide viable responses and explanations.

Depending upon the circumstances, it may also be possible for the chaplain to be active in organising visits to temples and shrines locally and, if possible, in India. Organising or conducting yoga and meditation sessions is another possibility, as is organising groups to meet with sadhus who visit the West. Chaplains will need to use their ingenuity and talent to seek out ways of inspiring spiritual development and creating environments in which constructive study and learning can take place. There are several bodies and community groups that can assist in this task, and it is a good idea to build up a range of useful contacts.

The situation for young people in diaspora communities is particularly pressing with regard to study and understanding of the tradition they have been born into. Most will have been educated to a high standard in Western schools and colleges and will therefore think intellectually in a manner that accords with Western culture rather than that of India. This means that their approach to the religion will be rather different to that of earlier generations, and will raise questions to be answered. One Indian woman reported: 'When we were young, we asked our parents "what" questions, but our children ask us "why" questions and we just don't know the answers.' Clearly there is an important function here that the chaplain can try to fulfil in providing the answers to those 'why' questions and, more generally, offering a broad philosophical discourse that will satisfy the inquiring minds of educated young people and convince them of the inherent value of their own traditions.

Hinduism has traditionally not placed a great emphasis on textual study, at least for most people, but in the West, and increasingly in India as well, knowledge of Hindu scripture and philosophy is being sought. In earlier centuries, knowledge of this kind was largely the preserve of brahminical communities, but in modern times we are witnessing a democratisation of religious and scriptural knowledge. This process, however, is by no means easy. A genuine understanding of the Hindu religious tradition requires an appreciation of the complexity of the subject and of the range of perspectives taught. If chaplains are to be an effective conduit of such knowledge then, again, we see the necessity of acquiring a sophisticated and wide-ranging knowledge of the various manifestations of Hindu spirituality and the relationship that exists between them.

Exercises

1. How valuable is knowledge of Hindu philosophy for the chaplain who is attempting to provide a coping strategy?
2. Discuss the best methods the chaplain can employ in order to avoid spiritual stagnation, and to create opportunities for learning.

APPLYING THE EPICS AND OTHER NARRATIVES TO SPECIFIC CASES

The extensive Sanskrit works known as the Mahabharata and Valmiki Ramayana are often referred to as the Hindu epics, although the term epic is not entirely appropriate, as above all else these two texts are scripture with all that this designation entails. Both were probably composed over two thousand years ago, although Western scholarship usually regards the Mahabharata as a composite work with different sections dating from different periods, hundreds of years apart. This view has never been proven and some major scholars do not accept it. The Hindu view is that the Mahabharata was composed by Vyasa in a period of remote antiquity, and the Ramayana composed by Valmiki in a previous age of humanity.

When Hindus refer to the Ramayana, they usually think they are talking about Valmiki's composition, but in fact this great literary work is only rarely read verse by verse, at least by the majority of Hindus. Nonetheless, the stories of the Ramayana are widely known in most communities, this knowledge coming primarily through film, television, dramas, dances, and storytellers. In most cases these are based on the version of the Ramayana composed in Hindi by Tulsidas about five hundred years ago, and Tulsidas's exposition is rather different from that of Valmiki. Moreover, we must also be aware of the oral traditions surrounding the Ramayana, so that narratives and events known to many Hindus will not be found in any of the written versions we possess today. Hence when we talk of the Ramayana we should be aware that we are speaking of a broad tradition rather than of a specific written work.

That tradition is focused on the person of Rama, who in classical Vaishnavism is regarded as an avatar, or descent, of Vishnu. Tulsidas and many of the northern traditions regard Rama as the supreme deity in his own right, with Vishnu as a secondary manifestation of Rama. In either case, the point would be that Rama is God in human form, and hence an object of love, devotion, and worship. The central narrative tells of Rama's marriage to Sita, his loss of his throne and banishment from his kingdom, his life as a forest dweller, the kidnapping of Sita by the evil Ravana, and the triumph in battle of Rama over Ravana, before his return to the city of Ayodhya where he was born, and where he rules as a perfect king.

This, of course, is only the briefest summary of the epic narrative, and ignores the numerous tales and sub-plots that surround the central story. At the risk of a gross oversimplification, we might observe that the principal religious themes of the Ramayana are the importance of making dharma central to one's life, and then devotion to Rama as the one supreme deity. In Valmiki's work, the emphasis on dharma is constantly to the fore, whilst the divinity of Rama is kept in the background, and is only occasionally referred to. For Tulsidas, and the wider Ramayana traditions, however, it is Rama's divine identity and the devotion due to Rama that form the central theme, and we are constantly reminded that although at times Rama acts as a human being, he is never subject to the exigencies of the human condition, remaining constantly in transcendence.

Hence for the chaplain, reference to the Ramayana can be used in these two broad lines of discussion. Valmiki's representation of dharma is relatively simple, positing a clear and straightforward dichotomy between virtue and iniquity. Central to this discourse are the person of Rama himself along with his dark antithesis, Ravana, the lord of Lanka. Where dharma, or the right course of action, is discussed, it will often be useful to cite examples of Rama's conduct as represented in the Ramayana, particularly in relation to his abnegation of material prosperity in order to maintain the precepts of dharma as the central pillar of his life. Ravana, by contrast, provides us with a valuable example of the forces that bring us to deviate from dharma. Ravana is not a fool, and neither is he irreligious in a formal or ritual sense, but a burning lust after material enjoyment seems to compel him to abandon any sense of righteousness, and to cause pain and suffering to others. He is the archetypal powerful man, who loses all concern for the rights of others, and in this way serves as a powerful warning to all of us who seek to implement the precepts of dharma in our own lives.

Moreover, the Ramayana offers us several other characters that can provide examples and illustrations of the forces that act on human beings. We have the filial loyalty of Bharata, the loving partnership between Sita and Rama, the manner in which Kaikeyi is tempted by the words of Mantara, or the conduct of Vibhishana who forgoes his own family for the sake of dharma and devotion to God. A detailed knowledge of the Ramayana narrative will undoubtedly assist chaplains in their work, particularly as these stories are widely known in most Hindu communities. The Ramayana's vision tends to be based on a simple dichotomy between good and evil, and draws much of its power from that division, but at the same time the divine identity of Rama, and the devotion offered to him as the supreme deity, could be seen as detracting from his position as a role model for humanity. Hence it may be that the other characters provide a richer source of inspiration for any consideration of human virtue and morality.

The Mahabharata, by contrast, presents us with a rather more subtle exploration of dharma, and the central characters are all too human in their struggles with life's dilemmas. The Mahabharata is a much longer and more complex work than the Ramayana, although it explores some of the same major themes, including the ideal of dharma, and devotion to God who takes on a human form as Krishna. Hence we can again assert that two of the major religious themes are dharma and devotion to God, but in addition the Mahabharata also offers a huge range of direct teachings on theological, ethical, and philosophical issues. A rough assessment would be that around one third of the text is given over to such teachings, although very few of them will generally appear in the abridged versions that are most widely available. The only complete English translations are those produced by Kisari Mohan Ganguli in the nineteenth century, still available in twelve volumes from Munshiram Manoharlal Publishing House, and a newer translation by Bibek Debroy.

Where the Mahabharata considers the subject of dharma, generally through its narrative and character representations, it repeatedly poses the question of how it is possible to adhere constantly to virtue whilst remaining active in a world beset by vice. The precepts of dharma are clearly stated, as we have seen, but how practical is it to adhere constantly to these precepts (in the manner that Rama does in the Ramayana, for example)? Central to this line of discourse, is the character of Yudhishthira, the most righteous of all the characters, the dharmaraja who finds it impossible to deviate from the path of virtue. Yet, despite his elevated character, we are shown that at times this constancy in the pursuit of dharma causes trouble to himself and to those around him, and we are drawn to the more robust and perhaps more practical approach advocated by his younger brothers, Bhima and Arjuna.

Alongside Yudhishthira, we have his wicked antithesis, Duryodhana, who consistently advocates the view that self-interest and ambition must take precedence in human life, and that dharma is simply a means of gaining worldly success. Then we have Dhritarashtra, an essentially righteous man whose virtue succumbs to the force of family affection despite the warnings repeatedly given to him by his brother, the wise Vidura. From the female side, we can observe the conduct of a number of women who are both virtuous and wise; Gandhari who seeks to restrain her husband's folly, Kunti who constantly serves and supports her sons and receives their love and devotion in return, and the beautiful Draupadi who has the learning and intellect to repeatedly engage in philosophical and ethical debate. These and other characters, and the numerous incidents that occur within the narrative, can all be used to add richness and interest to conversations, and the chaplain should see the text of the Mahabharata as an invaluable resource to be drawn upon for counselling purposes.

As in the Ramayana, a second principal theme is that of the existence of the supreme deity, and his manifestation as an avatar in this world, in this case as Krishna, who plays a significant role throughout the central narrative. Whereas Rama acts as a clear exemplar of ideal human conduct, Krishna appears as a rather more complex manifestation of the supreme deity. Within the narrative, Krishna tends to share the views of Bhima and Arjuna, and take a pragmatic rather than dogmatic attitude toward the implementation of dharmic principles. However, he also manifests his divine identity at various points in the narrative's progression and delivers a number of passages of religious instruction, the best known of which is the Bhagavad-gita.

In addition to the Bhagavad-gita, the Mahabharata also contains many extensive passages of religious and philosophical instruction, which all too often, unfortunately, remain overlooked by academic scholars of the Hindu tradition. For example, it is within the twelfth book of the Mahabharata that we find the earliest known teachings on *samkhya* and yoga, and later in the same book we find an extensive passage of early Vaishnava teachings, known as the Narayaniya. Perhaps paradoxically, there are also important expositions of early Shaivism also located in the later books of the Mahabharata.

A detailed knowledge of the content of both epics will be of enormous value to Hindu chaplains, although given the vast extent of both works, acquiring such knowledge will require a good deal of time and devotion. Some may perhaps feel that such ancient texts are of little relevance for the modern world, but nothing could be further from the truth. Both epics explore the nature of humanity and the problems of life that all people must confront. The answers provided are not always easy to comprehend, and the Mahabharata in particular is often equivocal in its explanations. But human existence is complex, and a more simplistic approach would inevitably be inadequate. Moreover, devotion to Krishna and to Rama are two of the most significant strands of Hindu religious tradition today, and for any discussion of these forms of spirituality, a detailed knowledge of the Mahabharata and Ramayana will be of immense value.

Perhaps most significantly, knowledge of these great works, and the teachings they offer humanity, will enable chaplains to enhance and augment any presentation they make, or any form of discussion they take part in. A purely theoretical form of discourse may be worthy, but any points made will be clearer and more potent when illustrated by examples taken from sacred texts that are widely known and widely revered. It is for this reason that we have repeatedly emphasised the importance of study for the Hindu chaplain, not just of the texts themselves but, where available, of courses and books that provide a deeper insight into their religious and ethical significance. Later on, we will provide an introductory course of study focused on the Mahabharata and Ramayana, which will give a solid basis from which to pursue further research into these two vitally important works.

Exercise

1. Select one episode from one of the epics (you need only refer to it briefly) and explain how chaplains might use this passage in their work.

VIEWS ON EXPRESSIONS OF FEELINGS

Much of this discussion must be based on cultural rather than religious considerations, and this in turn draws us into a consideration of rapid cultural change, both in India and amongst diaspora communities. Even in traditional Hinduism, there are variations to be aware of, especially with regard to contact between men and women. In most parts of India today, physical contact between unmarried men and women is disapproved of, and when one observes groups of young people they will tend to be segregated along gender lines. By contrast, within these single-gender groups physical contact is more acceptable than is usual in Western countries, where cultural restraints, particularly for young men, make what is deemed to be excessive physical contact unacceptable.

Sexual ethics in India would be considered rather conservative by Western standards, and young women in particular are very anxious to avoid any kind of reputation for promiscuity. Films may present a rather different picture, and the film actors may have a very different lifestyle, but traditional values still have a strong influence over many communities in India. Rapid cultural change is now exerting a considerable influence over many of these communities, as with those in the Western world, and this is causing a number of tensions to arise. In the West, we will encounter issues of generational conflict, with young people sometimes feeling they have to conceal aspects of their lives from their elders. This situation is by no means universal, and many parents and grandparents have accepted the need for cultural westernisation. Attitudes toward daughters' conduct, however, still tend toward conservatism, and this can give rise to feelings of guilt and even alienation amongst young women who wish to follow a lifestyle that does not accord with the views of the older generations. Issues over marriage can still occasionally arise, although in the West this is now very rare, and free choice is the norm.

A major problem that has emerged in India is the attitude of young men toward women who have adopted Western styles of dress and lifestyle and indeed toward women in general. High profile rape cases have drawn attention to this issue worldwide. The essence of the problem seems to be that a section of male society refuses to accept that Westernisation is not to be understood as a decline in moral standards. This product of rapid cultural change, coupled with the behaviour of a small section of male society, is causing problems throughout the developing world, and needs to be understood in its proper context.

The general rule is that Hindu culture dictates that physical contact between men and women should be confined to marriage partners, and this would include embraces or friendly kisses on the cheeks between friends of different genders. At the extreme, women were sometimes confined in the home so as to avoid interaction with other men. Similar issues may come to the fore in a professional setting, and here the receiving of medical examinations is a particularly salient point.

In Western societies, Hindu men and women are far more open to physical contact than has traditionally been the case in Indian society. It is now quite commonplace for men and women to greet one another with a light embrace or kiss on the cheek, although the acceptability of such gestures cannot be taken for granted, and some women may be offended by it. It is the younger generations in particular who are open to contact of this type, and it seems likely that this is a trend that will continue in the future in both India and the West. In terms of sexual behaviour, it is still very much the case that Hindu communities in the West have a great deal of respect for the institution of marriage, and that divorce still carries some degree of stigma. Amongst young Hindus, however, the situation is changing rapidly and pre-marital sexual relationships are now commonplace, although these may be kept secret from parents and elders of the family and community.

Such dissonance of values may well give rise to difficulties within families, and this may be an issue that chaplains have to confront within the context of their work.

The examination and treatment of female patients by male doctors has for some time now been an issue for families of an Asian background. When we consider Hindu communities located in the Western world, we will find that attitudes are usually more liberal and pragmatic than is typical of Islamic or even Sikh communities, and here again the issue of rapid cultural change amongst younger generations is significant. The point for chaplains to make on both these issues is that prohibitions of the types of physical contact we have referred to here are more cultural than religious. Hindu religious teachings emphasise the moral problems that arise from unrestricted desire, including sexual desire, and they insist on the importance of marital fidelity between partners, but such rules are clearly based on the ethical precepts of Sanatana Dharma that we have already considered in some detail. A chaste kiss on the cheek or an examination by a medical practitioner does not violate these precepts in any way, and therefore there is no reason for a devout Hindu to be offended by such circumstances. We should not, however, simply ignore the importance of cultural sensibilities, which for many Hindus are still of paramount significance and are closely associated with religious piety. Hence where chaplains find that such issues of physical contact are problematic, then they should adopt a sympathetic tone and try to do whatever possible to alleviate the difficulty, without attempting to pass judgement.

The chaplain's task in confronting issues such as those referred to above can be a difficult one. There may be times when one finds oneself caught between two family members and having to find a way to give proper advice to both whilst maintaining confidences. The key is to maintain strict adherence to the precepts of dharma in one's advice, whilst seeking to find a resolution that will bring the best possible outcome for all parties. Respect must always be given to the religious and cultural sensibilities of all parties. Dharma must always be given priority, but the importance of a respected neutral voice cannot be overstated, and this may well be another task for the chaplain.

Exercise

1. Discuss the significance of changing sexual ethics amongst young Hindus in diaspora communities. How does this affect the chaplain's work as religious guide and counsellor?

CONCLUSION

In the appendix, we have Ramesh Pattni's article on Hindu psychology. There is a lot of detail here, but if you are interested in this subject and wish to embark on further study, the article will serve as an excellent source.

APPENDIX: CHAPLAINCY AND APPLIED HINDU PSYCHOLOGY

By Dr Ramesh Pattni

WHAT IS HINDU PSYCHOLOGY

By Hindu psychology we mean an approach to psychology that is within the framework of concepts and practices developed over thousands of years within the Hindu traditions in India. This approach encompasses the underlying philosophy, conceptual and methodological frameworks, and the various 'technologies of consciousness', including meditation, that have been employed to bring about psychological change within the individual. The purpose of this change is to bring about certain states of mind which lead the individual toward, what is conceived by Hindu thought, as the ultimate purpose of human life. We can discern three unique aspects of such a psychology: firstly, a well-developed and sophisticated meta-theoretical framework; secondly, a rich base of psychological theories and thirdly, based on these principles, a wide array of psychological practices which not only take care of negative states of the individual but provide pathways toward a positive psychology that enhances health and well-being. It must be recognised that there are many different and complex voices within the Hindu tradition and it would be naïve to delineate one approach or paradigm as defining a Hindu psychology. Such a diversity of philosophical thought does not preclude us from finding common threads within this rich variety of expression. As the most often quoted aphorism says: *ekam sat vipra bahudh vadanti* – 'the truth is One but the wise call it by many names'. This points to a deep psychological understanding of the human mind and condition that the perception of reality is beyond any mental construction and the perception of this reality is constrained by the limitations of the individual's capacity and inclinations.

The Hindu metaphysic starts with radically different ontological and epistemological assumptions about the human being compared to the Western intellectual traditions. The most important ontological category is the transcendental reality which may be interpreted in different ways by the traditions. In other words, there are levels of non-physical existence not available for direct perception in the ordinary states of consciousness but which have a direct bearing on human experience and subjectivity, individually and socially. The causal networks extend far beyond one's physical reality and therefore the psychological status and states of the individual cannot be reduced to just physical or mental factors. Similarly, epistemologically, the intellect and the rational processes are to be cultivated in a certain way (*viveka*) but other sources of knowledge are acknowledged where there is a direct intuitive perception of the truth. Objective sense based knowledge is considered as one form of knowledge and even ignorance (*avidyā*).

Psychological practices within Hinduism sometimes tend to focus on yogic and mediation techniques although beyond these formalised practices there many different ways in which the psychological aspects of the individual can be managed or developed. Externally, the positive relation between a guru and a disciple can become a major way in which the inner 'tuning' of the disciple can take place leading toward an inner balance and harmony. The scriptures on the other hand contain instructions on the development of desirable inner attitudes, beliefs, and concepts that contribute to the development of a refined and subtle (*sāttvic*) nature for transcending beyond the limited ego individuality: non-judgemental self-observation; aspiration toward and a surrender to that which can be conceived as the highest or divine; transacting in the world with skill and equanimity, letting go of the fruits of the action and consecrating actions to the divine.

In summary, Hindu psychology starts with a different assumptive base to explain the nature and experience of the human individual and asserts the existence of dimensions beyond the physical reality that have a direct bearing on one's immediate existence and experience.

HINDU IDEAS OF PERSONALITY AND ITS EXPRESSIONS

Within the Hindu traditions we find a rich variety of conceptions and systematic analysis of the individual personality and the inherent mental and psychological processes. As we have pointed out, this is generally within context of goal of life which is the attainment of Realisation on the one hand and to release oneself from the cycles of birth and death (*samsara*). Each tradition offers a methodology for the control of the mind and its various cognitive, affective, and volitional elements. The psychological disciplines which engender spiritual development are again diverse and complex but follow the underlying philosophical assumptions of each tradition. This is again another unique feature of the Hindu psychology – mapping a course of spiritual development (*anubandha* and *anusāśana*) through psychological practice, whether it is the control of attention or inclination or attitude. There are several theories of personality within Hindu psychology, for example, the *nyaya-vaiseśika* or the *sāmkhya*-yoga, and although it is beyond the scope of this article to discuss these in detail, we give a glimpse of these before turning to consider the Vedanta one in more detail.

The *nyāya* and *vaiseśika* considers the cosmos, including the individual as constituted of nine categories (*padārtha*) including for example, substance (*dravya*), attribute (*guṇa*) activity (karma). The human personality consists of three primary factors: *atman* (soul), *manas* (mind) and śarira (body). The latter includes the five organs of action (*karmendriya*) and five organs of perception (*jñānednriya*). The *sāmkhya* and yoga traditions postulate the two reality principles of *prakṛti* (primordial materiality) and *puruṣa* (primordial consciousness) of which the former is the basis of all objective existence, both physical and mental, and consist of the three strands of *guṇa* (*sattva, rajas,* and *tamas*) which are in perfect equilibrium before manifestation. When there is a conjunction (*samyoga*) of the two principles, the sentient *puruṣa* and the insentient *prakṛti*, the conscious individual comes into existence who has the psycho-physical consisting of thirteen elements: *buddhi* (intellect), *ahamkara* (ego), *manas* (mind), the five organs of perception and five of action. The yoga tradition itself has a sophisticated and complex model of the mind designated as *citta*, which is like psychic machinery driven by subliminal factors of *samskāra, vāsanā,* and karma. The whole thrust of yoga practice defined in the methodology of *aṣtānga* and *kriyā* yoga, is to reach a state of cessation of the modifications of the mind (*citta vṛtti nirodha*) whereby the destination of *kaivalya* is attained and the pure consciousness (the seer) stands in its own nature. Let us see a more detailed analysis of personality from the Vedanta perspective.

Personality in Vedanta

The individual or *jiva* according to Vedanta can be described as consisting of the three bodies (*sarira*) or the five sheaths (*koṣa*) which are the components through which the personality expresses itself. These are adjuncts (*upādhi*) of that which is the essential truth of oneself – the pure consciousness of Brahman. The ego individuality comes into existence when the consciousness gets identified with these adjuncts through ignorance or *avidyā*. Through spiritual practices, one uncovers the truth of one's identity with Brahman and is no longer subject to the limitations of the adjuncts which, together with *avidyā* are the sources of all suffering in life. The identification with the body, mind, and intellect leads to bondage through attachment and results in the cycles of birth and death.

The individual accumulates karma through these many lives when identified actions are carried out in the world with a sense of 'I am the doer and I am the enjoyer'. Karma is the consequence of actions which are carried out with identification and attachment and this karma becomes the seed of future experiences and conditions in subsequent lives. Each individual has a storehouse of karma accumulated from all past lives (*sançita*) which is the source of karma in a particular life (*prārabdha*). The way in which one conducts one's life with the *prārabdha* karma becomes the source of future karma (*āgama*). The idea of karma is central to the meaning given to one's life and its unfolding circumstances which provides the basis for an individual trying to understand the source of one's life experiences. It is also key to the prescriptions which are provided by the philosophical systems to, on the one hand, manage the experience of current karma and on the other hand manage the creation of future karma conducive to a meritorious life.

Another key concept to consider is that of *vāsanā* which are inclinations and tendencies created by the impressions (*samskara* to which one is continuously subject to in each life. These *samskāra* crystallise into various traits which make up the personality. The texture of the *vasana* in an individual determines the way in which they function in the world and Vedanta provides a basis on which the personality can be typified according to this texture. Krishna in the Bhagavad-gita speaks of the fourfold division of personality types based on the attributes of nature (*guṇa*) and karma. The *guṇas* on one's nature are an expression of the texture of one's *vāsanā* – a preponderance of *sāttvic vāsanā* gives a brahminical disposition reflecting in someone who is intellectually inclined and interested in the pursuit of knowledge and its expression in life. A *rajasic* disposition with preponderance of *rajasic vāsanā* but with a fair amount of *sāttvic guṇa*, gives the *kshatriya* personality which is focussed on action and leadership in the protection and preservation of society. A combination of *rajasic* and *tamasic guṇa* gives the *vaiśya* personality inclined toward commerce and a life based on accumulation of material wealth. The physically inclined person has a large share of *tamasic guṇa* and functions mainly at this level.

The equipment through which the personality expresses itself is modelled as the three bodies or *sariras*: the gross body (*sthula śarira*) consisting of the five organs of perception and five organs of action and is the interface between the inner and the outer world; the *suksma sarira* or the subtle body consists of the *buddhi* (intellect), *manas* (mind), *citta* (memory or conditioned consciousness), and *ahamkara* (ego, or sense of 'I'). These four factors are also called the *antahkaraṇa* or inner instrument; the *kāraṇa śarira* or causal body is where the *vāsanā* and karma are said to be located and as these are the cause and expression of one's current life, it is called the causal body.

Vedanta also accepts the five levels or sheaths of the personality. There is also correspondence between the threefold body and the fivefold sheath models. The five sheaths are also considered as levels of personality expression and related to the psychological functioning of the individual. These five sheaths are described as follows:

1. *The annamaya kośa*

This is the food (*anna*) sheath and is composed of the food ingested by the individual transforming into the material physical body. The body is born out and grows out of the food taken by the parents and transformed into the foetus growing on the food ingested by the mother. This *kośa* is the physical aspect of the personality through which it expresses in perception and action in the outer world.

2. *The prāṇamaya kośa*

Also known as the 'vital air sheath' it is the location and activity of the five *prāṇa* or vital airs which control the physiological functions of the physical body. They are also the link between the physical and the mental as the state of the *prāṇa* affects not only the body but also the mind. The five *prāṇa* are *prāṇa, apāna, vyāna, samāna, and udāna*, each of which has a specific function. *Prāṇa* is related to the respiratory system and which is said to move upwards; *apāna* corresponds to the excretory system and moves downwards; *vyāna* is said to be linked to the whole organism and related to the nervous and circulatory system; *samāna* is related to the digestive system; *udāna* is related to the head and the neck, and is said to govern speech and creative thought.

3. *The manomaya kośa*

This is related to the *manas* or mind. It is the level of processing emotions and also said to control the operation, through the *prāṇa*, of the physical body and senses. It is the sheath where the sensations from the sense organs come together to form perceptions for further processing by the next sheath – the *vijñānamaya kośa*.

4. *The vijñānamaya kośa*

This is related to the intellect and functions to process the thoughts with discriminative intelligence, knowing, analysing, judging, and making choices. Its function is affected by the *manomaya koṣa* which can create powerful emotions that override the reasoning capacity of the intellect.

5. *The ānandamaya kośa*

This is also known as the bliss sheath and is nearest in proximity or subtleness to the *atman*, the centre of one's being, which is the same as Brahman, according to Advaita Vedānta. In this sheath it is the bliss of the *atman* which is reflected but conditioned by the past experiences of the individual. This becomes externalised and objectified as search for happiness in the external world of objects, beings and situations.

The five *kośa* which function as the levels of personality, reflect also its integrity. When they are aligned, the individual functions effectively in the world and the greater the alignment with the true purpose and meaning of life, the greater the sense of well-being and health which is experienced. The Hindu texts make reference to this in many ways and in many places for example, when the personality is aligned to doing *punya* (meritorious acts), and living a life of dharma through thought word and deed. This process of alignment of the *kosha* or the fine-tuning of the three bodies, are preparations for the fulfilment of life's purpose as liberation or intense devotion to God in selfless service. From the Hindu perspective, the sense of well-being and happiness comes from turning towards this 'higher' purpose through the paths of yoga as described in the Bhagavad-gita. Here we see the clear link between psychological well-being through the methods of spirituality and these prescriptions for the ills and suffering of the individual, are clearly set out in the texts. These are also the links between the phenomenal identity functioning in the world, and the transcendental Reality which is to be realised as the truth.

Hindu philosophy also describes the four areas of effort which the individual exerts in his or her life. These are the four *puruṣārtha* of dharma (righteous action), *artha* (material gain or gain of that which is considered of value), *kāma* (expression of passions) and *mokṣa* (gaining liberation), which are expressed in different proportions in each individual. They also set out the way in which the balanced life is to be lived: the gain for material wealth and the expression of one's desires are to be done within the boundaries or context of dharma and moksha. It defines one's relationship with the world and the direction of one's effort in each stage of one's life. There are four stages which are described in the scriptures: *brahmaçārya* (stage of learning and discipline);

grahaṣtha (stage of the householder); *vānaprastha* (stage of turning away from the householder's duty and focus on one's spiritual life, literally meaning 'staying in the forest'); *sannyās* (the stage of renunciation of worldly life for a spiritual life). The psychological counselling in broad terms therefore relates to not only the constitution or temperament of the individual but also the stage of life one is in. Let us look in more detail as to what this counselling may involve.

HINDU VIEWS ON PSYCHOLOGICAL COUNSELLING

If the prescriptions of the scriptures are the means to aligning or fine tuning the personality then this is the context within which one can consider psychological coaching or counselling. The methods prescribed have to do with the management of the individual at various levels of being and experience, and are means of purification of the individual of the ego-centric identity and attachment. Whether it is the body, the mind or the intellect, there are appropriate practices given which turn each aspect of oneself toward the divine and the higher purpose of one's existence. The idea however is not the development of the personality for its own ends, for secular gains, but rather prepare the individual for self-transcendence. Psychological counselling within the Hindu context therefore focuses on relief from suffering through spiritual means, turning the individual to the ultimate purpose of life through practice (*abhyāsa*) and detachment (*vairagya*). *Abhyāsa* is that practice which is done for the right reasons, over a long period of time without a break and with full dedication and *vairagya* is detachment from all that is peripheral to the ultimate purpose of life. We will now consider some broad aspects of psychological counselling from the Hindu perspective. We have already noted models of the individual and personality and seen how these can be considered as heuristic in the sense of being practically oriented toward the spiritual goal of life. So for example, the theory of the *guṇas* of nature is used to explain how there is a transformation of the *guṇas* as one progresses in one's spiritual life and by what means this transformation can be effected. Implied in what we have said is the Hindu view that the essence of one's being is happiness and suffering is due to the ignorance of this true nature. This is, in contrast to the view that life is a constant struggle for survival and that suffering is at the root of life and living. The view one takes, of course, informs the counselling process which is adapted and is based on the underlying metaphysical understanding of life and the individual. The role of the counsellor is to provide the framework and the means of relieving the suffering of the individual through whatever is appropriate to the client; and from the spiritual point of view, the counsellor will awaken the suffering person to his or her own true and essential nature. Here it is understood that one of the roles of the chaplain is counselling and the person who is being counselled will be referred to as the client, who may be so in various settings – whether in hospital or university, care home or a prison.

This however may not be the direct approach which is taken up by the counsellor or the chaplain who is sitting in front of the inmate in a prison or the patient in the hospital. The client is led through a reflective process which takes the present condition and experience of the client analysing them through the cognitive framework of Vedanta. Thus there is a dialectic process which corrects the 'cognitive error' – taking the world and the ego identity to be real – through the experience and condition of the person. The interpretation and explanation of the experience, in other words, is within the spiritual framework and the precepts of Vedanta. Whether it is explained in terms of the impermanency of life events, the continuation of the *jiva's* journey through its allotted *prarabdha karma*, or whether it is shown as an opportunity for spiritual growth through present suffering, the counsellor will take the person through this corrective process. The scriptures may be quoted to assist in the understanding of the experience.

There are however some difficulties which could be inherent in this approach. Firstly, it assumes that a capacity in the client to engage in an intellectual process which leads toward changing the view of one's condition. It may be argued that this capacity may not be available to everyone but on the other hand, the analysis of the immediate experience is much more direct than other means and therefore effective in bringing about the change. Secondly, it assumes that the counsellor has the spiritual knowledge and the experience to engage with the client in an effective manner. This is an important consideration and points to a training programme for someone who wishes to work with Hindu clients. It should be noted that despite these constraints, it is still possible to achieve change in the client through this approach.

Bhagavad-gita and counselling

There is a life-affirming positive approach given in the Hindu scriptures which goes beyond the negation of suffering. It shows the pathway whereby life can become positive, peaceful, and joyous through the reframing of one's perspective according to the precepts of the scriptures. We will now look at a specific text which can clearly be considered as positive in its approach – the Bhagavad-gita – and consider its implications for counselling. The vision of the Gita is expansive in terms of what it encompasses. The immediate dilemma of Arjuna in the battlefield and the experience of his crisis at a critical point in his life is the ground in which this vision is rooted whereas it expands to a consideration of the highest spiritual truths that have a direct bearing on this immediate experience on Arjuna. The Gita is often considered as a manual of life and living and gives the ultimate spiritual solution to the challenges of the transactional life. Krishna is the divine counsellor who engages with Arjuna, the human 'client' and the discourse can be considered as Arjuna's treatment for this existential condition. There is, in other words, a rich psychological content in the Bhagavad-gita which provides the basis of Krishna's analysis of Arjuna's condition and lifts him to a greater vision within which the solution to his condition is given. We have already given some idea of the Vedanta model of the personality and this is considered in detail in the verses of the Gita. In fact, many of the verses of the Bhagavad-gita can be utilised for counselling and often we find that during bereavement, the Gita becomes the text of choice in the public prayers and eulogies as well as a means of giving support through the verses of the Gita, to those who have been bereaved. The grief of loss in death and the grief of Arjuna in the battlefield come together in the precepts of the Gita which define the fundamentals of the human condition and provide the ultimate prescriptions for dealing with suffering arising out of it. Let us consider some of these precepts and see how they relate to psychological counselling.

Firstly, the immediate counsel of Krishna to Arjuna is to recognise the truth of one's being – the unchanging, imperishable, eternal *atman*. This at once changes the perspective of the individual from the ego identified transient personality to the eternal *atman* which has assumed a transient body for the purpose of discharging its *prarabdha karma*. This doctrine of the eternal *atman* experiencing the limited human condition has had a tremendous impact on the Hindu psyche throughout the ages and even today it is the most effective counselling frame for pain, suffering, death, and grief. Most Hindus turn to the Gita in times of crisis and find strength and solace in its words. If one asks the question why one should not grieve over those who have died or about to die, Krishna replies that: 'Never was there a time when I did not exist, nor you, nor these rulers of men. Nor, verily, shall we cease to exist in the future' (2.12). When the physical body dies, the self or *atman* that has enlivened the body does not cease to exist. It is imperishable an eternal and the Vedas proclaim: 'Thou Art That'. Therefore, why grieve? Here we see that the counsel is not related to finding a psychological solution to the grief but reframing the problem and giving it a spiritual solution.

Secondly, the Gita insists that action in life is unavoidable and if this is the case then it means one has to do the best one can with the right consciousness. Everyone is engaged in action and this will result in many different experiences – pleasure and pain, joy and suffering, honour and dishonour. Each circumstance or situation can be looked at from three viewpoints and depending on the perspective, so can our response and our experience. One can react from the ego identity and get affected according to one's conditioning; or one can take a spiritual perspective and look at the situation from this point of view. Throughout the Gita, these two perspectives appear again and again and are reconciled through its prescriptions. If the true nature of the world and one's own self is understood and is clear, one will be able to put life and its challenges in the proper perspective. The counselling approach is to point toward the right perspective, away from the ego identity and toward one's spiritual self and to view the difficulty one is facing from this perspective. Thus the Hindu view on counselling is to achieve this cognitive shift through the methods for example, of the Gita, which specifies the three paths of yoga for this purpose. This shift results in equanimity and skill in action raising one beyond the contingent dilemmas and challenges of life.

Thirdly, actions require choice and the problem of choice confronts all humanity as it did Arjuna. In a sense Arjuna's crisis is about the crisis of choice – he says he does not know what to do. Krishna gives him the basis on which the choices are going to be made. He explains to Arjuna that right action requires right thinking and this is done within the framework of truth, which also gives the goal of life to be pursued. This goal, according to Vedanta, is to pursue the Truth, whether this is in a name and form as Ishvara or nameless and formless as Brahman, whether it is immanent or transcendent. Realising the truth is the highest goal and when everything is clearly seen within this goal, choice and action become consistent and the personality gets integrated in the truth. For the counsellor then, the task is to bring this integration about through clarification of the goal, the turning towards that goal, a growth in commitment to the goal and practical means of expressing that commitment. With these steps, the resolution of the client's problem becomes possible and the pathway to freedom from suffering becomes clear.

This in brief is the way the Bhagavad-gita takes the psychological being in its condition of suffering and gives it the spiritual solution that fundamentally resolves the human condition by lifting the vision to the highest Truth. The counsellor through the means stated above takes the client through a widening and deepening of the consciousness and reflecting together on the client's experiences, brings clarity to the goal and the means to reach it. In a sense this relationship is reminiscent of the guru-disciple relationship, although in practice it works out in a much narrower sense. It is focussed on resolution of the client's condition and is time-bound with boundaries set on the relationship in terms of what needs to be achieved and how. The goal of counselling from the Hindu perspective is to guide the client in his or her journey toward the truth. The immediate challenge or crisis is only a catalyst toward growth and by facing it equipped with the knowledge and the wisdom of the scriptures and the guidance given by the counsellor, both spiritual and psychological maturity is gained. The goal of counselling is to remove the discord that arises from the misperception of one's true nature and the misidentification with one's transient individuality. The task of the counsellor is to take the client on a journey of self-discovery that leads to an end to suffering and the experience of harmony and joy. We will discuss the specific pathways of the Gita in the next section.

HINDU RELIGIOUS COPING

People respond to threats to their mental and physical well-being with coping behaviour. Coping behaviour can be defined as ongoing cognitive and behavioural efforts to manage specific external and/or internal demands that are appraised as taxing or exceeding the resources of a person. This response is triggered by 'coping appraisals' that judge the confronting event as stressful and could represent a threat of harm or loss, challenge with possibility of growth, or something beneficial. The central qualities of coping can be considered as:

- an encounter between a person and the situation;
- multidimensional, multi-layered, diverse contextual phenomenon and,
- possibilities and choice.

Another way of looking at coping is to consider it as a continually changing process through which individuals try to understand and deal with significant personal or situational demands in their lives. Here the key assumption is that there is some coherent orienting system which individuals have that provides a way in which they perceive and deal with the world. If then religion is a way in which people attribute meaning and purpose to life, i.e. a coherent orienting system, then religion becomes a way of dealing with life's difficulties. The conceptual basis for religious coping is not only linked to major theories in psychology such as attachment and attribution, but also specifically, coping theory as well. Religious coping occurs when goals and means, events and circumstances are actively appraised in relation to the sacred, which in turn enhances the sense of meaning, control, intimacy and support. The outcome of religious coping can be judged to be good or bad according to whether it meets the demands of the situation. Three primary types of coping can described: (1) emotion-focused coping which involves changing attention away from the distress causing emotions to the problem or meaning of what is happening; (2) problem-focused coping which involves engaging with the environment or the self and trying to change what is causing the distress; (3) religious coping which involves the use of religious practices and beliefs in response to the perceived stress. There are cultural differences in coping methods used by individuals for example, Western culture tends to value problem focused coping over other methods whereas the Eastern cultures tend to focus on religious methods. Three main styles of religious coping can be described as follows: (1) self-directed coping which acknowledges the presence of the sacred but relies on oneself rather than God to deal with the problem; (2) deferring coping where the responsibility is deferred to God; (3) collaborative style which involves an active partnership between God and the individual. Another broad classification which is used in research on religious coping is positive and negative religious coping, in which the former has a positive focus on solving the problem within the religious context and the latter involves a sense of religious discontent and lack of religious community support.

Religious coping as a means of dealing with a number of critical life situations has been correlated with health outcomes, both mental and physical in studies over the last three decades. These studies show that religion becomes a compelling resource for dealing with stressful situations. Although there is now a large body of evidence on the connection between religion and coping, there are limitations which are pointed out: limitation of explanatory power of the coping construct; coping theory is seen to be too simplistic and ignores many other factors important in the process of coping e.g. changes in coping process over time, and the multidimensional nature of religion .Many studies have been done on the relationship between religiosity, religious coping and psychological well-being and several mechanisms have been identified in these relationships:

- Meaning: Religion provides a way of making meaning of life.
- Control: Mastery and control over oneself and the world can be obtained through religion.

- Comfort: Anxiety can be reduced through religious practice.
- Intimacy: Closeness to God and people can be attained through religion.
- Life transformations: Transforming life through new significance derived from religion.

How do these ideas relate to Hinduism and what are the specific ways in which Hindus cope with life's challenges? What are the mechanisms and methods which the counsellor can equip the client for increasing the capacity to deal with ongoing challenges? We can look at some of the specific practices which are or can be used by the counsellor when dealing with the Hindu client.

Aṣṭānga yoga

Yoga can be considered as one of oldest system of holistic health in the world with its roots in Indian philosophy. Its significance and utility in mental health practice has been acknowledged throughout the world and is being used as an adjunct to psychotherapy and counselling in many countries. Yoga's central idea is one of union and through its practices, unites and harmonises various aspects of the individual: body, breath, mind, intellect, and consciousness. It has been established that yogic practices affect various systems within the body, relaxing the body, and bringing alertness and concentration in the mind and creating emotional balance. Patañjali who wrote the Yoga Sūtra in the 4th Century CE gives an eight limb methodology for preparing all the aspects of the individual for attaining altered states of consciousness leading to the realisation of *puruṣa* or pure consciousness – the state of *kaivalya*. The yoga sessions involve the practice of various physical postures, breathing exercises (pranayama), and different stages of meditation. The eight limbs of the Patañjali's astanga-yoga consists of *yama* (observances), *niyama* (restraints), *asana* (physical postures), *pranayama* (breathing exercises), *pratyāhāra* (inwards direction of attention), *dhāraṇā* (concentration), *dhyāna* (contemplation), *samādhi* (meditation). Each practice takes up an aspect of the individual and harmonises and integrates it with the others.

Several features of yoga make it an attractive option for treating psychological conditions. Yoga practice, including physical postures, yoga breathing, and meditation and guided relaxation have all been demonstrated to improve executive functions like manipulation of information in the verbal working memory, attention span and visuo-motor speed of the patients suffering from major depression. Yoga has been shown to improve social and occupational functioning, better adjustments to day to day life problems, positive outlook toward life, work, useful in reducing stress, improved mood, and improvement in overall quality of life. Yoga could bring significant changes in one's adjustment to life and provide coping mechanisms which can be used on a daily basis.

As an example let us look at practice of one of the limbs of the eight-limb yoga system: *pratyāhāra*. According to Patañjali, this practice is 'the state of disconnection of the contact between the sense organs and their respective objects. Regular control of *pratyāhāra* leads to attainment of greater control of the senses and leads to increased ability for complete attention and concentration'. Here the main effect of the practice is control of attention. When the attention is withdrawn from the sensory perceptions, the inward drawing of attention leads to awareness of the inner world. This can have two significant effects: firstly, the turning of attention inward leads to a greater inner awareness as an observer. This observer state results in a sense of detachment from the activities of the mind and this disengagement has been shown to lead to decreased anxiety. Secondly, with the holding of the observer state, there is the possibility of repressed and negative thoughts and feelings arising. If the impartial observation of the content of the mind is held while these come into awareness, there is possible a cathartic release from the memories. The job of the counsellor would be to guide the client through this process and help manage his/her anxiety as the content comes into awareness. Just this one yoga practice can be used in the counselling set up to gain significant results for the client. The other limbs of astanga-yoga can usefully be adapted to aid the therapeutic process.

Karma-yoga

We have already mentioned that the Bhagavad-gita centres around the crisis of Arjuna, and Krishna provide a spiritual solution to this condition of Arjuna. One of the paths advocated by Krishna is that of karma-yoga or selfless transacting in the world. We have noted that states of anxiety arise, as in the case of Arjuna, when there is attachment to the results of one's actions. In life one is oriented externally to the world for the fulfilment of one's desires. This sets up a cyclical process of subliminal inclinations expressed as desire in the mind leading to actions in the world with expectation of a certain result. In Chapter 2 of the Gita the 'ladder of fall' is illustrated by Krishna as follows: dwelling on an object leads to attachment and desire and for the object; this results in anger and frustration; from anger arises delusion and from this the loss of memory; discrimination becomes ineffective when memory and past wisdom is lost; when discrimination of right and wrong, good, and bad is lost, the person 'perishes'. Krishna goes on to say that the person of self-control and discipline, moving amongst the objects, with the senses under control, free from attraction and repulsion, attains peace and serenity.

Here we can see the Gita's analysis of the roots of anxiety and agitation in the mind that takes away inner balance with a loss of inner peace. This analysis points to two things: egocentric desires which lead one down the ladder of fall, and secondly the collateral aspect of desire – expectation of, and attachment to, a certain result. This orientation of the person toward fulfilment of desires and attachment and that creates constant anxiety in the mind is countered by the twin principles of karma-yoga: dedication of all actions to God and accepting the results of actions as the gift and grace of God. This re-orientation from ego-centrism to God-centrism of the client can be assisted by the counsellor although it would be one of the long-term strategies for health and well-being. It also encompasses the dharma as the fulfilment of one's duties and responsibilities according to one's stage and station in life. Karma-yoga in a sense is the practice of dharma without expectation and attachment and this orientation helps the clients to focus on performance of duty and action to the best of their abilities.

Bhakti-yoga

The second key aspect of the Krishna-Arjuna dialogue centres on divine love and the how surrender in this love leads toward right relationship with transactions in the world. *Bhakti,* or devotion, is stated as seeing the beloved in everything and everyone. 'Whatever you do, whatever you eat, whatever you sacrifice, whatever you give, in whatever activity you are engaged in, do it as an offering to Me' (9.27). Not only does such an approach in life lead toward surrender to the divine but one gets liberated from the bonds of action, explains Krishna. A person who surrenders to the divine finds refuge and comfort in the divine and this leads to the mind becoming centred and calm in the thought of the divine. This relationship of love with the divine also creates an explanatory base from which the circumstance of one's life and condition can be made sense of; there is meaning derived from such a relationship which can have a positive and powerful effect on the mind through acceptance and surrender. The task of the counsellor is then to turn the mind of the client toward the divine through various means so that the divine in a chosen name and form becomes the object of one's attention. This can be done through prayer, chanting of the name, through rituals or puja and through contemplation on God. In fact the nine modes of devotion which are described in the Ramcaritmanas of Tulsidas as well as Bhagavata Purana, give a set of therapeutic tools for counsellors. In the Ramcharitamanas, Rama gives Sabari the *bhakti* path consisting of nine modes:

1. *satsangh* – company of like-minded individuals;
2. *katha sravanam* – revelling in the stories of the divine;
3. *guru-seva* – service to the guru;
4. *kirtanam* – singing the glories of the divine;
5. *japa and bhajan* – chanting and singing the name of the Lord;
6. *dharma* – self- control and following the righteousness of the sages;
7. *samdarsana* – seeing the Lord in all;
8. *santosha* – being content with what one has, and;
9. *saralta* and *sraddha* – straightforwardness and steady faith in Me.

(Aranya Kanda 15/16)

The Bhagavata Purana gives a different version of the nine forms of devotion:

1. *sravaṇa* – listening to the stories of Krishna;
2. *kīrtana* – praising and singing together;
3. *smarana* – remembering or fixing the mind on Vishnu;
4. *pādasevanam* rendering service to the Lord;
5. *arcana* worship;
6. *vandana* prostrating and paying homage to the Lord;
7. *dāsyam* relating to the Lord as his servant;
8. *sākhyam* relating to the Lord as friend, and;
9. *ātmanivedana* self-surrender

(Bhagavata Purana, 7.5.23–4)

The role of prayer, chanting of mantra and singing the glories of the Lord are considered to have a significant effect on the mind and these are often advised as ways in which one can come to terms with challenges and losses in one's life.

Jñāna yoga

Jñāna is knowledge and the path of knowledge is described in the scriptures as one using the methods of knowledge leading to establishment in the truth of oneself. In the context of counselling from this perspective, we can consider the characteristics of the person who is a *sthita-prajñā*, one who is of steady wisdom or the one who has become established in the truth. The discourse given to Arjuna on this subject is given by Krishna at the end of Chapter Two of the Bhagavad-gita in what is known as the section on *sthita-prajñā-laksana* (2.53–72). This, in a sense, represents the goal of human life marked by contentment, peace, and happiness. If the distress of a person is arising because of the imperfections due to the non-establishment in the knowledge of the self, then this can be seen as the prescription to that condition. The human condition is graphically illustrated by Vidura to Dhritrastra in the Mahabharata (Book 12 section 5/6) form which we consider in the following section.

He concludes 'the wise know life's course to be even such. Through knowledge they succeed in tearing off its bonds'. There are however problems with becoming established in the self: 1. ignorance of the self; 2. doubts and confusions about the self; 3. continuation of old patterns of thinking and action which prevent the knowledge of the self. The path of knowledge prescribes a three stage process for overcoming these problems: 1. *sravanam* – listening to discourses and discussion on the self; 2. *mananam* – reflecting on that which has been heard; 3. *nidhidhyasanam* – removing old patterns of thinking through contemplation on the self. In the Brihadaraynaka Upanishad (2.4.5), Yajnavalkya tells Maitreyi: 'The self should be seen, heard, reflected on and contemplated upon. By seeing, listening, reflecting, and contemplating, all is known'. In the Gita (2.56) Krishna describes the person who has become established in the truth of his/her self: 'He whose mind is not shaken by adversity and who in prosperity, does not hanker after pleasures, who is free from attachment, fear and anger, is called the sage of steady wisdom'.

The human condition, if it is subject to sorrow and suffering, can be transformed through right knowledge according to the Gita. The three categories of sorrow mentioned in the scriptures are:

- *adhibhautika* – arising from the surroundings, their origins being known; they may arise from the neighbourhood, family members, creatures, bacteria, etc.
- *adhidaivika* – arising from the elemental forces: earthquakes, torrential rains, cyclones, and fires
- *adhyātmika* – arising from our own self, *vyadhi* which is physical; *adhi* which is mental and *upādhi* – intellectual dilemmas

Krishna's prescription of establishment in steady wisdom takes care of these sorrows which arise in the human condition: the mind does not become shaken by adversity nor does it hanker after pleasures in prosperity; there is freedom from attachment, fear, and anger and therefore the mind becomes calm and steady. The task for the counsellor is therefore threefold within this approach through the path of knowledge:

1. Guided listening to the knowledge of the Self, providing the client with the resources that he/she can read, listen to or watch;
2. guided reflection on the meaning of that which has been listened to in order that meaning may be derived from that which has been listened to;
3. guided meditation on the knowledge which has been reflected on.

In summary, there is a raft of techniques available to the counsellor from the scriptures which can be highly effective in terms of dealing with the condition of the client. These techniques deal with the whole person from the physical to the emotional, from the intellectual to the spiritual and bring about the relief of suffering. The counsellor will be guided according to the evaluation of the client in terms of his/her current experiential state and will be able to guide the client in using the most appropriate method. We now consider another rich source of therapeutic value – the Hindu epics, for example the Ramayana, the Bhagavata Purana, and the Mahabharata.

ROLE OF HINDU EPIC NARRATIVES IN COUNSELLING AND CHAPLAINCY

One of the basic accepted principles of psychotherapy and counselling and underlying their practice, is that verbalisation of experience has a significant therapeutic effect. With the attentive trained ear of the counsellor, the clients, when speaking about their problems, come to terms with them. This principle however was not always accepted and it was during the1980s that scholars such as Jerome Bruner and Donald Polkinghorne brought the study of the narrative into focus. It became apparent that the arrangement of events into an internally coherent sequence, in which each succeeding event is causally related to the preceding ones, had a therapeutic power. Also contained within this idea of emplotment or the coherent sequence of events, is that of the relationship between the narrative and selfhood. This reflects the postmodern idea that there are multiple identities created in the course of life and the elicitation of these diverse identities in coherent whole is the basis of the therapeutic effect. Conflicts and trauma when disclosed in this way have a tension releasing effect which results in improved physical health as well as sense of well-being.

Another principle related to narrative therapy is that there are some ways of narrating that are more therapeutic than others. When for example, with the narration, deep emotions are identified, expressed and explained in relation to an overall narrative and sense of selfhood, there can be a much stronger therapeutic effect than just a simple narration of events. In the late 1980s and early 1990s Michael White and David Epston, proposed that the 'problems experienced in people's lives were not simply located within themselves, as indissoluble parts of their person, but rather derived from the ideologies and culturally sanctioned stories prevalent in society'. From this point of view the religious narrative can be seen as that which speaks to the roots of one's identity and culture and can be powerful in their effects on the individual who engages with them through faith in the tradition. The listening of such stories opens up a space for reflection allowing the reframing of one's own narrative and sense of selfhood which can lead toward release from entrenched and unproductive ways of being toward a new sense of agency and empowerment.

The distance created between the person and the issue explored through the use of metaphor and the narrative implies learning to separate content from process; clients can step back and view themselves. Using the metaphor of a bicycle, clients can envision the path they have taken, where they are at the moment, and where they want to go. By reviewing the contents of their lives, they can come to understand their actions and their meanings. This enhanced capacity for self-reflection enables them to actively respond to situations, not merely react to them. In other words, therapeutic efforts with clients are grounded in an understanding of the character of human existence and the narrative is a mode of thought that links together a set of life happenings or choices as they hinder or contribute to an outcome. It grasps life as movement through time in which actions are directed to desired ends. It is the mode of thought through which we understand ourselves and others. It is about understanding the human condition and the Hindu scriptures and particularly the epics have a dramatic way of expressing this condition. Here is an example from the Mahabharata one of the best known epics of Hinduism.

Let us take an example of a narrative in the Mahabharata which is about the Kuru dynasty. Vidura who is learned and wise tells his half-brother, Dhritrastra, the blind king who has asked him about the human condition:

> I will obey thy behest by telling thee how the great sages speak of the wilderness of life. A certain brahmin, living in the great world, found himself

on one occasion in a large inaccessible forest teeming with beasts of prey. It abounded on every side with lions and other animals looking like elephants, all of which were engaged in roaring aloud. Such was the aspect of that forest that Yama himself would take fright at it. Beholding the forest, the heart of the brahmin became exceedingly agitated. His hair stood on end, and other signs of fear manifested themselves, O scorcher of foes! Entering it, he began to run hither and thither, casting his eyes on every point of the compass for finding out somebody whose shelter he might seek. Wishing to avoid those terrible creatures, he ran in fright. He could not succeed, however, in distancing them or freeing himself from their presence. He then saw that that terrible forest was surrounded with a net, and that a frightful woman stood there, stretching her arms. That large forest was also encompassed by many five-headed snakes of dreadful forms, tall as cliffs and touching the very heavens. Within it was a pit whose mouth was covered with many hard and unyielding creepers and herbs.

The brahmin, in course of his wanderings, fell into that invisible pit. He became entangled in those clusters of creepers that were interwoven with one another, like the large fruit of a jack tree hanging by its stalk. He continued to hang there, feet upwards and head downwards. While he was in that posture, diverse other calamities overtook him. He beheld a large and mighty snake within the pit. He also saw a gigantic elephant near its mouth. That elephant, dark in complexion, had six faces and twelve feet. And the animal gradually approached that pit covered with creepers and trees. About the twigs of the tree (that stood at the mouth of the pit), roved many bees of frightful forms, employed from before in drinking the honey gathered in their comb about which they swarmed in large numbers. Repeatedly they desired, O bull of Bharata's race, to taste that honey which though sweet to all creatures could, however, attract children only. The honey (collected in the comb) fell in many jets below. The person who was hanging in the pit continually drank those jets. Employed, in such a distressful situation, in drinking that honey, his thirst, however, could not be appeased. Unsatiated with repeated draughts, the person desired for more. Even then, O king, he did not become indifferent to life. Even there, the man continued to hope for existence. A number of black and white rats were eating away the roots of that tree. There was fear from the beasts of prey, from that fierce woman on the outskirts of that forest, from that snake at the bottom of the well, from that elephant near its top, from the fall of the tree through the action of the rats, and lastly from those bees flying about for tasting the honey. In that plight he continued to dwell, deprived of his senses, in that wilderness, never losing at any time the hope of prolonging his life'.

Vidura said, 'That which is described as the wilderness is the great world. The inaccessible forest within it is the limited sphere of one's own life. Those that have been mentioned as beasts of prey are the diseases (to which we are subject). That woman of gigantic proportions residing in the forest is identified by the wise with decrepitude which destroys complexion and beauty. That which has been spoken of as the pit is the body or physical frame of embodied creatures. The huge snake dwelling in the bottom of that pit is time, the destroyer of all embodied creatures. It is, indeed, the universal destroyer. The cluster of creepers growing in that

> pit and attached to those spreading stems the man hangs from is the desire for life which is cherished by every creature. The six-faced elephant, O king, which proceeds toward the tree standing at the mouth of the pit, is spoken of as the year. Its six faces are the seasons and its twelve feet are the twelve months. The rats and the snakes that are cutting off the tree are said to be days and nights that are continually lessening the periods of life of all creatures. Those that have been described as bees are our desires. The numerous jets that are dropping honey are the pleasures derived from the gratification of our desires and to which men are seen to be strongly addicted. The wise know life's course to be even such. Through that knowledge they succeed in tearing off its bonds.'

One can see that this is a powerful story which puts the human condition into perspective and we can discern several aspects of this story which highlights the use of such stories in counselling.

Therapeutic effects of narratives: We have noted the effects that a narrative can have in terms of one's sense of identity and one's own story. Listening to a story one re-experiences the thoughts and feelings of the actors in the story and in an appropriately chosen story, there is identification with a particular character. This identification with its concomitant experience of the state and the story of the character, when it is verbalised through the intervention of the trained counsellor gives rise to several results. Firstly, it creates the space within which unexpressed or even unidentified emotions and thoughts and mind-sets are brought into awareness. Secondly, the awareness of one's own inner condition in relation to the perceived outer condition with the guidance of the counsellor can begin the process of meaning-making about one's own condition. Thirdly, the meaning-making itself results in understanding and acceptance of one's situation leading finally toward adjustment and adaptation with the newly gained insight. It is important to remember that narratives can be powerful initiators of inner processes and requires the careful guidance of the counsellor in giving the right direction to these processes. Also the counsellor needs to be familiar with the epic stories of which there are numerous examples in the texts, which can have be useful in the therapeutic setting. For example, the story of Hanuman in the Ramayana is often used to build confidence and self-esteem and deal with anxieties and fears in one's life. Additionally the counsellor needs to have his or her own insight into the narratives so that the guidance to the client becomes effective within the overall framework of Hindu thought.

Narrative catharsis

What we have mentioned above is the process of what can be called catharsis which occurs with the telling and discussing of the story from the epics. Catharsis is a word of Greek origin which means purification or purgation, especially of emotions. In psychology it was Freud who developed the 'cathartic treatment' for patients suffering hysterical symptoms, through hypnosis. The term catharsis has also been adopted by modern psychotherapy, particularly Freudian psychoanalysis, to describe the act of expressing, or more accurately, experiencing the deep emotions often associated with events in the individual's past which had originally been repressed or ignored, and had never been adequately addressed or experienced. One can see how through the process of identification in listening to the narrative that one can experience deep emotions which can be the starting point of healing of oneself and one's relations.

Inspirational and healing messages

Narratives in the epics contain many healing messages and these are often quoted even in ordinary conversations to bring perspective and wisdom to understanding life and life situations. An example of this is in the Ramayana: The Vibhishana Gita is considered to be a portion of the *Lanka Kanda* of the Ramayana (79–81) when in the middle of the battlefield Vibhishana becomes disconcerted on seeing Ravana his brother on a chariot and Rama without one. He speaks to Rama, his heart filled with tenderness: 'My Lord, you have no chariot, nor any protection for either your body or your feet, how can you hope to conquer this mighty warrior Ravana?' Rama tells him that the chariot which leads one to victory is quite another and outlines the necessary tools for human beings to complete the voyage of life safely and to attain spiritual progress and mental purification. Rama takes the metaphor of the chariot and gives the context in which one must live one's life for life's voyage on this chariot:

> Valour and fortitude are the wheels, truthfulness and good conduct are its banner and standard, strength, discretion, self-control, and benevolence are its four horses, and the reins are forgiveness, compassion, and equanimity of mind; adoration of God is the expert driver, dispassion the shield and contentment the sword; charity is the axe, reason the fierce lance, highest wisdom the relentless bow; a pure and steady mind the quiver, while quietude, restraints, and observances the sheaf of arrows; Homage to one's teacher is the impenetrable coat of mail. One who owns such a chariot shall have no enemy to conquer anywhere.

Wisdom and experience of characters

Through the characters of the epic one can derive wisdom, and their experiences can be mirror images of one's own life experiences. One often finds that one gets identified with certain characters in the epics whether it is Sabari or Sita, Rama or Kevat, Arjuna or Bhima. Living the lives of these characters through the telling and retelling of their stories becomes a way of reflecting and internalising the wisdom of their lives with positive therapeutic consequences and a reworking of one's affective relations.

Positive narrative energies

Narratives often create positive energies reflecting the expression of the archetypal characters, metaphors, and symbol in the stories of the epics. The qualities of servant leadership which are displayed for example by Hanuman can become instruments of inspirational change within one's life. The counsellor's task is to find the relevant energies required by the client's current condition and identify the appropriate character or episode which brings a change in energy of the client.

BIBLIOGRAPHY (TO APPENDIX ONE)

Anderson, R, The Search for Spiritual/Cultural Competency in Chaplaincy Practice: Five Steps that Mark the Path, Journal of Health Care Chaplaincy, 13:2, pp 1–24, 2004

Balodhi, J and Keshavan, M, Bhagavadgita and Psychotherapy, Asian Journal of Psychiatry 4, pp 300 - 302, 2011

Beckford, J, Doing Time: Space, Time Religious Diversity and the Sacred in Prisons, International Review of Sociology: Revue Internationale de Sociologie, 11:3, pp 371–82, 2001

Byrd, J. STM, Chaplaincy, Gerontology & Geriatrics Education, 1:2, pp 129–32, 1981

Carey, L, Newell C, and Rumbold B, Pain Control and Chaplaincy in Australia, Journal of Pain and Symptom Management, Vol 32, No 6, 2006

Ching-Huang Wang, Yi-Jou Lin, Yu-Chen Kuo & Su-Syuan Hong, Reading to relieve emotional difficulties, Journal of Poetry Therapy: The Interdisciplinary Journal of Practice, Theory, Research and Education, 26:4, pp 255–67, 2013

Cornelisson, M, Misra, G, and Verma, S, Foundations of Indian Psychology, Pearson, New Delhi, 2011

Dalal, A and Misra G, Core and Context of Indian Psychology, Psychology and Developing Societies 22, 1, pp 121 – 15, 2010

De Castella R, and Graetz Simmonds, J, 'There's a deeper level of meaning as to what suffering's all about': experiences of religious and spiritual growth following trauma, Mental Health, Religion & Culture, 16:5, pp 536–56, 2013

Emery, E, Who am I with Parkinson's Disease? A Psychologist Response to Chaplain Intervention in the Context of Identity Theory, Journal of Health Care Chaplaincy, 19:3, pp 120–29, 2013

Galek, K, Flannelly, K, Koenig, H, and Rev. Fogg S, Referrals to chaplains: The role of religion and spirituality in healthcare settings, Mental Health, Religion & Culture, 10:4, pp 363-377, 2007

Gangadhar, B, Bhagavadgeeta: The Indian treatise on mental health care and promotion, Asian Journal of Psychiatry 4, p 303, 2011

Gilbert, P, Seeking inspiration: the rediscovery of the spiritual dimension in health and social care in England, Mental Health, Religion and Culture, 13:6, pp 533–46, 2010

Harding, S , Flannelly, K , Weaver, A, and Costa, K, The influence of religion on death anxiety and death acceptance, Mental Health, Religion & Culture, 8:4, pp 253–61, 2005

Harlow, R, Developing a spirituality strategy – why, how, and so what?, Mental Health, Religion & Culture, 13:6, 615–24, 2010

Ingemark, C (Editor), Therapeutic Uses of Storytelling: An Interdisciplinary Approach to Narration as Therapy, Nordic Academic Press, 2013

Joshanloo, M, Eastern Conceptualizations of Happiness: Fundamental Differences with Western Views, J Happiness Studies, 15:475–93, 2014

Kelly, E, The Development of Healthcare Chaplaincy, The Expository Times, 123(10), pp 469–78, 2012

Kumar, A and Kumar, S, Karma yoga: A path towards work in positive psychology, Indian J Psychiatry. Jan; 55(Suppl 2): S150 – S152, 2013

Kuppuswamy, B, Elements of Ancient Indian Psychology, Konak Publishers, India, 1990

Levitt, H , Rattanasampan, W , Chaidaroon S, Robinson C, The Process of Personal Change Through Reading Fictional Narratives:

Implications for Psychotherapy Practice and Theory, The Humanistic Psychologist, 37:4, pp 326–52, 2009

Loewenthal, K, A Short Introduction to the Psychology of Religion, Oneworld Publications, Oxford, 2000

Masson, J, Indian Psychotherapy? Journal of Indian Philosophy 7, pp 327–33, 1979

Mundle, R, Religious Pluralism and the Hospital Chaplain, Scottish Journal of Healthcare Chaplaincy, Vol 12, No 2, pp 16–20, 2009

Neki, J, Psychotherapy in India: past, present, and future. Am. J. Psychotherapy, 29, January (1), 92–100, 1975

Orton, M, Transforming Chaplaincy: The Emergence of a Healthcare Pastoral Care for a Post-Modern World, Journal of Health Care Chaplaincy, 15:2, pp 114–31, 2008

Paranjpe, A, Theoretical Psychology, the meeting of East and West, Plenum Press, NY, 1984

Paranjpe, A, Theoretical psychology: The meeting of east and west. New York: Plenum Press, 1984

Ramachandrarao, S, The conception of stress in Indian thought, the practical involvement in Gita and Ayurveda. Nimhans J. 1, 123–31, 1983

Rao, K, Paranjpe, A, and Dalal, A, (Editors), Handbook of Indian Psychology, Cambridge University Press, India, 2008

Rao, K, What is Indian psychology? Journal of Indian Psychology, 7(1), pp 37–57, 1988

Ruffing, J, To Tell the Sacred Tale: Spiritual Direction and Narrative, New Theology Review, pp 38–52, August 2009

Sharma, R, Hindu Techniques of Mental Health, Shubhi Publications, Delhi, 2000

Snyder C and Lopez S (Editors), Handbook of Positive Psychology, Oxford University Press, New York, 2002

Thillainathan, N, Four Paths to Freedom, Hindu Concepts in Counselling, Psychotherapy in Australia, Vol 16 No 3, May 2010

Walsh, R, Two Asian psychologies and their implications for Western psychotherapists, American Journal of Psychotherapy, XLII: pp 543–60, 1988

Worthington, E, Kurusu, T, McCullough, M, Sandage, S, Empirical

Research on Religion and Psychotherapeutic Processes and Outcomes: A 10-Year Review and Research Prospectus, Psychological Bulletin, Vol. 119, No. 3, pp 448–87, 1996e

www.ingramcontent.com/pod-product-compliance
Lightning Source LLC
LaVergne TN
LVHW020713110826
845149LV00012B/2250

* 9 7 8 1 9 9 9 7 6 4 4 0 1 *